BASSES AND GUITARS

The Huckabee Collection

By
WILLIE G. MOSELEY

Foreword by James Burton

Acclaim Press
— Your Next Great Book —

P.O. Box 238
Morley, MO 63767
(573) 472-9800
www.acclaimpress.com

Book & Cover Design: Rodney Atchley

ISBN: 978-1-956027-37-2 | 1-956027-37-8
Library of Congress Control Number: 2022945225

Photos by Willie G. Moseley unless otherwise noted
Front cover photo courtesy of TBN
Back cover photo (Gov. Huckabee) courtesy of TBN
Author photo by Elizabeth Moseley

First Printing: 2022
Printed in the United States of America
10 9 8 7 6 5 4 3 2 1

This publication was produced using available information.
The publisher regrets it cannot assume responsibility for errors or omissions.

CONTENTS

In memory of Dimitri Polizos and Barry Bailey

My father was right—make friends with a Greek, and you've got a friend for life.

And the friendship with Barry was a bonus for which we were both grateful.

FOREWORD

Of all the people Mike knows, I am truly honored that he asked me to write the foreword in this book.

We have known each other for years, and I've been on his television program many times, and man, the talent he has never ceases to amaze me.

No matter what song we play together, Mike plays it well, with very little rehearsal. That's the sign of a true musician.

If you've seen and heard him play, you know what I'm talking about—Mike takes care of business.

Mike also takes his guitars and basses seriously and after you read this fantastic book, you'll have a new appreciation for his talent, his love for music, and his awesome collection of stringed instruments, including a Red Paisley Flames Telecaster... like mine.

I know that you will enjoy these pages as much as I do.

Keep on playing!

— *James Burton*

Courtesy of TBN

INTRODUCTION

Many observers of the contemporary news media are used to hearing elected officials pontificate in a loud and boisterous manner.

But don't expect any high-decibel bombast or "where's-the-camera" histrionics out of the former governor of Arkansas.

On his television show and elsewhere, Mike Huckabee presents his well-informed point of view in a reasoned, non-confrontational and conversational style, without finger pointing at a guest who might have an opposing perspective. He'll stick to his guns about a particular issue that he supports or opposes, but he won't get in his guest's face about it. The evolution of his "Everyman" approach has resulted in a style that ordinary folks have come to appreciate in the years that Mike's been in the public arena.

And ordinary folks should be able to appreciate his collection of basses and guitars, as well.

Actually, Mike's musical experiences aren't particularly rare or unique, nor is his interest in instruments with which he came of age in the late '60s and early '70s. As of this writing, Baby Boomer males are still the driving force in the vintage guitar phenomenon, in spite of graying demographics and the effects of the COVID-19 pandemic.

Huckabee's assemblage of stringed instruments isn't comprised of high-priced collectibles of a certain brand, or certain models in certain finishes. Nor are they a lineup of "look-what-I've got" items. Some of them are budget instruments that were used for autographs.

And another percentage number regarding how he acquired his instruments is impressive—two thirds of the basses and guitars he owns were given to him.

This is a "people's collection" that includes a lot of "people's instruments," and there are plenty of "people stories" to go along with many of them.

And that's exactly the way Mike Huckabee envisioned this presentation.

LEXICON

ARCH-TOP: Somewhat self-explanatory; some hollow or semi-hollow instruments have a curved/contoured top that is sometimes carved. The term is usually associated with guitars rather than basses, and isn't necessarily used when discussing solidbody instruments, although "carved top" *is* used regarding solidbody instruments (see separate definition).

BINDING: Material that is usually made from flexible plastic; "binds" edges of wood together, but sometimes its use is strictly cosmetic.

BRIDGE: Metal, wood, or plastic part on the top of an instrument where strings "transmit" vibrations for sonic reproduction. A bridge usually has small grooves in it to accommodate each string. Many bridges have adjustable "saddles" for individual strings, to allow intonation/fine tuning. Most bridges on electric guitars and basses also have threaded bolts on either side to facilitate adjustment of string height.

BOLT-ON: Self-explanatory type of attachment of a neck to a body

BOOKMATCHING: Alignment of two or more matching pieces of figured wood in an opposite/reverse "mirror image" pattern along a centerline to create a desired aesthetic. This style is often seen in furniture construction on items such as dining room table tops and occasional tables. In guitar making, such patterns are usually seen on the tops of instrument bodies.

BOUT: Upper and lower portions of a standard-shape guitar or bass body, separated by an indention/"waist." The two sections have a connotation that implies viewing an instrument that is on display vertically—"upper bout" refers to the part of the body nearer to the neck joint, while "lower bout" refers to the portion nearer the end of the body, where the bridge, controls on electric instruments, etc. are usually found.

CARVED TOP: This term usually describes a contoured top found on many guitars and basses, including solidbodies. The carved top may be part of the same wood as the body, or may be a different wood that is attached.

"CASE CANDY": Items found in the pocket of a guitar case, including straps, strings, picks, song lists, cords, warranty cards, instruction manuals, etc.

CONTOUR: Beveling on solidbody instruments to enhance comfort. Such contouring often consists of a "belly cut" on the back, and a "forearm bevel" on the top—and both of those terms are self-explanatory. As noted earlier, "contouring" can also refer to a carved top on an instrument body.

CUTAWAY: Portion of guitar or bass near neck/body joint that appears to have been cut out to allow access to higher area of the neck. Such shaping creates a "horn" on the body silhouette. Instruments may be single-cutaway, symmetrical double-cutaway or offset double-cutaway (most solidbody guitars and basses).

DREADNAUGHT: An acoustic flat-top guitar body style that has more of a "squared" silhouette with a shallower waist/indentations. First popularized by the Martin company.

FLAT-TOP: Another self-explanatory term. This is the classic configuration of an acoustic guitar.

"FLOOR-SWEEP": a term used to describe instruments that were made with leftover parts, just to use up such items. While such guitars and basses might be rare, there can be potential controversy over how collectable they might be, since many, if not most of them were pieced together in somewhat of a hodge-podge manner.

FRET: A metal strip on a fingerboard/fretboard. Each space between frets serves the same sonic function as a piano key by changing the pitch of a string by one note. The metal strips that delineate each space are usually made of "fret wire," an alloy.

FRET MARKERS: Also known as "position markers". Decorative dots, blocks or other inlay on the fretboard playing surface and/or side of the neck for visual reference.

FRETBOARD: Also known as a "fingerboard." Top surface of a guitar or bass neck where notes are selected and played. Rosewood and ebony are among the most popular fretboard woods laminated to the top of a neck. A maple fretboard is often part of a maple neck itself instead of being a laminated part.

HARDTAIL: A reference to a guitar that does not have a vibrato, while its standard configuration does feature a vibrato.

HEADSTOCK: Top end of instrument where the tuning keys and brand name are (usually) found.

JACK: Receptacle for guitar cord.

LUTHIER: An individual builder who hand-makes stringed musical instruments, usually in a small shop.

NAMM: Acronym for "National Association of Music Merchandisers," an organization of retail music businesses. New instruments and other musical wares usually debut at "NAMM shows", which are usually held twice a year.

NECK-THROUGH/NECK-THRU: A type of stringed instrument construction where the neck and center portion of a solidbody instrument are contiguous, and the other portions of the body are attached like "wings." Sometimes the neck-through portions is composed of laminated woods. A classic example of this configuration is the Rickenbacker 4000 bass series.

"NEW-OLD-STOCK": Guitar collectors' term for instruments or parts that have languished in storage or layaway for years without being sold or used. The abbreviation for such items, "N.O.S", is also cited in vintage guitar parlance.

NUT: Small grooved part for string spacing and height, located between headstock and fingerboard. Usually made of bone, plastic, metal, or, in more recent times, space-age composite material.

PICKGUARD: Somewhat self-defining item, usually made of plastic or metal, that shields a guitar or bass body from pick damage (if the player happens to use a pick); also known as a "scratchplate."

PICKUP: Microphone-like device consisting of a magnet or magnets and wiring that "picks up" string vibrations. "Single-coil" pickups have a self-explanatory designation, while "humbucking" pickups have two coils, wired in opposition to each other to cancel out annoying electrical noise.

"P/J": Abbreviation for a popular setup of pickups on basses, with one offset humbucking pickup, as found on a Fender Precision Bass ("P"), and one straight bar single-coil pickup, as found on a Fender Jazz Bass ("J").

POTENTIOMETERS: "Pots" aren't visible, but are critical to the function of an electric guitar or bass—they're the electronic controls underneath a volume or tone knob.

RADIUS: Arc/curvature of fretboard from one side to the other. Measured in inches (from which the radius is figured)—the smaller the number, the more pronounced the arc/curvature.

SCALE: Distance from nut to bridge. Scales found on most electric guitars are either 24 3/4 inches or 25 1/2 inches, both of which are considered industry standards. Bass scales are 30-30 1/2 inches (short), 32 inches (medium), 34 inches (standard or full), or 35 inches (long).

SET-NECK: Refers to the glued-in neck style found on some guitars or basses.

STRING TREE: Hardware attached to headstock to stabilize strings between nut and tuning keys.

TAILPIECE: Anchor point for "ball end" of string. Independent tailpieces are "stop"-type (attached to the top of the instrument) or somewhat-trapeze-shaped, attached to the bottom rim of a guitar body.

THINLINE: A hollow or semi-hollow guitar or bass configuration with a body that has a shorter depth (usually around two inches) than most acoustic stringed instrument bodies.

TOGGLE SWITCH: Turns individual pickups off and on. The most common configuration is found on a two-pickup instrument, with a three-position toggle switch that works either pickup individually or both at the same time. Toggle switches are also used to control other functions of a guitar or bass.

TRUSS ROD (and TRUSS ROD COVER): Most modern guitars and basses have a metal truss rod inside the neck to alleviate string tension (which, if not controlled, could cause the neck to warp). The truss rod is usually adjustable, and is accessed (depending on the brand and model) via a plate located on the headstock (just behind the nut/headstock juncture) or on the butt end of the neck.

VIBRATO: A device with an "arm" that is part of the tailpiece on some models. It is manipulated by a player's hand to change the pitch of a note or a chord on guitars or basses. Rapid manipulation results in a "warbling" sound.

ZERO FRET: An extra piece of fret wire positioned where the neck joins the headstock; utilized to facilitate better-sounding chords. Some luthiers will note that if a zero fret is found on a fretboard, the part that is normally referred to as a "nut" should be referred to as a "string guide."

1. BASS QUEST—A BRIEF HISTORY

It took three Christmases for Mike Huckabee to get his own electric guitar and amplifier.

Michael Dale Huckabee was born and raised in Hope, Arkansas, a small town in the southwest corner of the state. The community is noted for its watermelon crops and claims to be the home of the largest watermelon that has ever been grown (268.8 pounds, documented in 2005).

Hope was also the birthplace of Bill Clinton, forty-second president of the United States. Clinton and Huckabee are both former governors of Arkansas, and Huckabee has run for president twice.

Mike's parents, Mae and Dorsey, were traditional-values folks who had to monitor their family finances closely. As children during the Great Depression, they had learned practical frugality the hard way, and they referenced such real-life experiences when their own adulthood arrived. Dorsey would be compelled to work two jobs, as a fireman and an automobile mechanic. Their daughter Pat was two years old when Mike came into the world on August 24, 1955.

Mike established an interest in guitars early on and would recall that it was the only musical instrument he wanted to learn to play. A family photo shows him at age five, manipulating an inexpensive Sears Supertone Round-Up brand cowboy guitar owned by his father; if displayed vertically, the instrument would be almost as tall as Mike himself. The illustration on the guitar's top is a stenciled Western motif that includes the signature of movie star Gene Autry.

Huckabee was eight-and-a-half years old when, like millions of other Americans, he watched the Beatles on *The Ed Sullivan Show* on Sunday, Feb-

Mike with his father's "cowboy guitar" (age five) — Courtesy of Mike Huckabee

Mike with his Vox Clubman Bass and Silvertone amplifier. His Penncrest 1580 guitar sits on a stand; it was sold soon after this photo was taken.—Courtesy of Mike Huckabee

ruary 9, 1964. He was fascinated by the original compositions of the band—the Beatles proffered snappy, melodic pop songs on jangly guitars played by George Harrison and John Lennon, as Paul McCartney anchored the proceedings with innovative bass lines and drummer Ringo Starr maintained the tempo like a human metronome.

Ultimately, the Beatles' appearance on *The Ed Sullivan Show* would be cited by many historians and music fans as the most important and/ or memorable event in pop music history. The band would be hailed as the frontline aggregation that abruptly wrenched the American popular music scene out of the doldrums of its teen idol era, in which it had floundered for a number of years. Other bands from the United Kingdom quickly became part of what was dubbed the British Invasion.

And like a myriad of other youngsters, Mike began pestering his parents for an electric guitar.

"Christmas 1964, couldn't afford it; Christmas '65, couldn't afford it," he said of his pursuit. "I didn't give up, and they were finally able to get me one for Christmas of '66, when I was eleven years old."

Mike's new guitar was a definitive example of the budget facet of the fabled guitar boom of the 1960s. His Penncrest (J.C. Penney house brand)

guitar had been made by the Kay company of Chicago. The Huckabees opted for a special $99 package deal that included the guitar, case, stand, and a small amplifier that was also made by Kay.

A Pentecostal minister was Mike's first guitar teacher. Blistered and bleeding fingertips were expected among neophyte guitarists, but Huckabee persisted in developing his skills. However, he quickly noticed that there was a dearth of electric *bass* players among his peers.

"There were guys who played guitar all over the place," he recounted, "but there were very few bass players. I figured that if I played bass, it would be easier for me to get a gig."

Accordingly, Huckabee soon acquired a short-scale English-made Vox Clubman Bass and a Sears Silvertone 1466 piggyback-style amplifier.

"The Beatles and other British bands were known for playing Vox amplifiers," Huckabee detailed, "so almost *anything* with a Vox label on it was cool."

The Silvertone 1466 was a solid-state amplifier made by the Danelectro company of New Jersey. Its looks were perhaps deceiving because its relatively small, no-frills amplifier head cranked out 150 watts, making it the most powerful Silvertone amp ever produced and marketed.

The speaker cabinet was 32 inches tall and was mounted on casters for easy conveyance. It housed six ten-inch speakers, and the amp head could be stored inside.

Huckabee sold his Penncrest guitar and amplifier about a year-and-a-half after he got them, in order to buy a three-pickup Vox guitar that resembled a Fender Stratocaster. However, he remained committed to playing bass with his adolescent musical peers. He listened carefully to bass lines in pop and rock songs, picking out the intricacies of low-end, single-note passages that had to be synchronized with a kick drum. He also developed a new list of musicians who influenced his playing style.

"Of course, everybody listened to [Paul] McCartney," he said, "but for me, there was also Chas Chandler of the Animals. His notes really stood out; he ended up becoming a big executive in the music business in England. I also liked the bass lines on some of the songs that Paul Revere and the Raiders did, especially one called 'Him or Me—What's It Gonna Be.'"

Huckabee's citation of the Animals is understandable, since two hits by that band, "It's My Life" and "We Gotta Get Out Of This Place," crank off with memorable solo bass riffs from Chandler.

English bassist Chas Chandler, as seen in an early publicity photo of the Animals—Wikimedia Commons

The Raiders and their employer on the set of Where The Action Is. Left to right, front: Paul Revere, Dick Clark, Mike Smith; back: Drake Levin, Phil "Fang" Volk, Mark Lindsey—Courtesy of Phil Volk

Moreover, Mike's attraction to the music of Paul Revere and the Raiders seems to help validate the assertion by bassist Phil "Fang" Volk in a 2004 interview that the Raiders and the Beach Boys were the only two American rock bands that successfully battled the bands of the British Invasion. Volk played bass in the "classic" lineup of the Raiders in the mid-'60s. The gig included a house band residency on a Dick Clark-produced weekday afternoon television show called Where The Action Is.

"I watched it every time it was on," Huckabee enthused. "They were really a great band."

At the advent of the '70s, Huckabee would become imbued with the loud, overdriven bass sound purveyed by Mel Schacher of Grand Funk Railroad, a Michigan band that epitomized the term "power trio."

Mike's love of music was further bolstered when he worked at a radio station part-time, starting in his early teens. He handled his responsibilities in a professional manner.

He had also become aware of the earliest music of the "Jesus rock" movement and considered singer/guitarist Larry Norman the progenitor of what would evolve into the Contemporary Christian Music (CCM) genre. The idea of performing faith-oriented music on (sometimes loud) modern instruments that were normally used by secular rock bands was innovative and appealing to many music

Grand Funk Railroad publicity photo, 1971. Left to right, Don Brewer, Mark Farner, Mel Schacher—Wikimedia Commons

Larry Norman, mid-'60s. Huckabee opined that this photo made Norman look like a doppelgänger of singer Peter Noone of Herman's Hermits.—Wikimedia Commons

fans—particularly teens—who liked rock and roll but were uncomfortable with some of the lyrics, as well as the lifestyles of some of secular music's frontline performers.

While in high school, Huckabee played in a combo that went by the cryptic/pseudo-artsy moniker of the Bois D'Arc Boogie Band. He also began participating in a great American pastime for guitarists and bass players, frequenting pawn shops on a regular basis in search of bargains on out-of-hock instruments.

Eventually, Mike became the owner of a late sixties Fender Jazz Bass in a sunburst finish and an early sixties dark cherry red Gretsch 6119 Chet Atkins Tennessean guitar. The Gretsch matched the instrument played by George Harrison in the Beatles' first movie, *Help!*

Following high school, Huckabee enrolled in Ouachita Baptist University in Arkadelphia, Arkansas. He and classmate Janet McCain, who had also graduated with Mike from Hope High School, were married at the end of their freshman year, in May 1974.

Huckabee would graduate with honors in three years, and the couple then moved to Fort Worth, Texas, for Mike's graduate work at Southwestern Baptist Theological Seminary.

Like many young couples, the Huckabees struggled financially, especially when they were in Texas. Janet had a malignant tumor on her spine removed, and their first child was born in November 1976.

Mike was compelled to sell all his instruments and gear to make ends meet. He fully acknowledged that family came first but resolved to re-acquire some decent and similar equipment sometime later, income permitting. In 1980, he managed to buy a Yamaha acoustic guitar from a pawn shop for $80, but his dry spell for owning several instruments, including a bass, would continue for many years.

When Mike became governor of Arkansas in 1996, he acquired a used Fender Jazz Bass (thanks to Janet) and promptly formed a weekend warrior-type band with other state officials called Capitol Offense.

"We came up with that name because we all worked at the Capitol, and our music offended a lot of people," he wisecracked.

Capitol Offense's part-time approach to the classic rock they purveyed didn't mean they were cavalier about their musical presentation, however. They honed their chops in a professional and dedicated manner and ultimately opened shows for Willie Nelson, Grand Funk Railroad, REO Speedwagon, and other notable bands and singers.

Huckabee would also play bass in the worship band at the church his family began attending when they moved to Little Rock. A friend had

Mike plays a Yamaha bass while sitting in with a worship band during a 2010 fundraising event in Iowa.—Wikimedia Commons

told him about a new start-up church that was meeting in a storefront. It would become known as the Church at Rock Creek and was pastored by Mark Evans.

"It had Baptist roots, but it was nondenominational," Mike explained. "When we got involved, it had about 60 people, and it still had folding chairs. What was important was the desire to reach across racial and economic lines, and it happened. You might see a bank president sitting next to a recovering addict, who was sitting next to an attorney, who was sitting next to somebody on welfare. The praise band needed a bass player, so I volunteered."

Later, Mike created an organization that donated musical instruments to underprivileged children. In 2010, he appeared on a benefit album titled *I Wanna Play! An Album To Put Musical Instruments Into The Hands Of Every Child In America* to support the initiative.

"We got people to donate instruments they weren't using," he said, "and we'd get them refurbished and would give them to kids that needed them."

Even as governor, Huckabee would still hit pawn shops on a regular basis, in search of collectible basses and guitars. It had to have been a startling sight to a hock shop employee when the governor of Arkansas walked into his/her store, perhaps accompanied by two state troopers.

"When I traveled, I'd still go to pawn shops—*always*," he averred. "Eventually, the Arkansas troopers knew to expect it, but if I was in another state, like maybe Texas, Louisiana, or Indiana, sometimes troopers would pick me up at the airport and ask me where I needed to go. You should have seen the looks on their faces when I said, 'A pawn shop!'"

Over the years, trips to campaign, give speeches, or participate in seminars or dedications over the years have often included opportunities to sit in with live bands that were performing at such events, and Huckabee has enthusiastically contributed low-end riffs with local musicians, using a borrowed bass.

Huckabee's weekly television show first aired on the Fox News Channel prior to his 2016 presidential campaign. As of this writing, the infotainment-format broadcast originates from the Nashville area on the Trinity Broadcasting Network (TBN) channel. Notable musicians from numerous genres have appeared on his program over the years, and Mike often sits in with the guest musician(s) at the end of the show. Guests have run the gamut from singer/activist Melissa Etheridge to veteran bassist Victor Wooten to bluegrass icon Ricky Skaggs to hard rock players like Phil Collen of Def Leppard and Brian "Head" Welch of Korn.

Mike's collection of basses and guitars is diverse for unique reasons. It makes sense, however, to begin a perusal of his instruments by examining the ones that have the most personal importance to him in chronological order.

2015: At a housing seminar at Saint Anselm College in New Hampshire, Huckabee played with country singer Ayla Brown, using what appeared to be a '70s Fender Precision Bass. Brown is the daughter of former Massachusetts US Senator Scott Brown.—Wikimedia Commons

An improbable-but-musically-viable collaboration between Brian "Head" Welch and the governor on the set of Huckabee's television show. Welch is playing a unique seven-string electric guitar, and that's the neck of Huckabee's custom-made Wilkins bass in the foreground.— Courtesy TBN

2. PERSONAL TIME (WARP) MACHINES

SEARS SUPERTONE ROUND-UP

Since Mike's earliest documented experience with a guitar was the photograph of him playing his father's Supertone Gene Autry Round-Up at age five, it was a given that he would like to acquire a similar instrument, and his unexpected acquisition of such a guitar occurred in Little Rock, on November 24, 2009.

Steve Evans was the proprietor of Jacksonville Guitar Center, just up the road from Arkansas's capital city. He had been in business since 1975.

"I started collecting vintage guitars when I first opened the store," Evans recounted, "and it turned into a great hobby for me. A main benefit was the ability to display them in my store."

Evans's business sold vintage cowboy guitars, among other styles, but he differentiated between instruments in his collection and instruments in his store inventory. At the assemblage's peak, he owned 150 traditional wooden models and 125 toylike instruments made from fiberboard, tin, and plastic.

His collection happened to include a 1934 Round-Up guitar, made by the Harmony company of Chicago and marketed by Sears Roebuck under the Supertone house brand. It was featured on p. 22 of *Cowboy Guitars*, a photo-centric book that was a collaboration between Evans and Ron Middlebrook, published in 2002.

"The Round-Up was not part of my merchandise," Evans clarified. "It was part of my collection."

Huckabee and Evans had already done business. As sitting governor in 2003, Huckabee had purchased a 1964 Gretsch Tennessean in Jacksonville (to be chronicled later in this chapter). A new friendship was forged, and the governor and the guitar dealer had kept in touch.

Huckabee's book *A Simple Christmas* was published in November 2009. The photo of him at age five with his father's Round-Up guitar was on the front cover. Evans decided to present his own Round-Up to Mike at a book signing in Little Rock.

"As I walked up to the front door of the bookstore with antique guitar in hand, I realized this was going to be either really embarrassing or pretty cool," said Evans. "Well, it was great! I had a good time visiting with the people in line, and when it was my turn to have my book signed, Mike was thrilled to see me, and he loved the guitar. I hadn't planned to let it go, but Mike was the right guy for that guitar.

"The next morning, I got a call from my daughter in North Carolina, telling me Mike Huckabee had just talked about our meeting on his radio show and had named me as Huck's Hero for the day. Holy mackerel!"

The Supertone Gene Autry Round-Up model was introduced in a Sears catalog in 1932 and had

This debut ad for the Gene Autry Round-Up guitar was seen in the Fall 1932 Sears catalog. Courtesy of Steve Evans

a mahogany body (back and sides) and neck. It featured a "selected clear spruce top". The body measured 13 inches wide on the lower bout. The ebonized fretboard had three dots.

By the time the Fall 1934 Sears catalog was published, the back and sides were mahogany-stained birch, and the neck also had a mahogany finish (and may have been birch as well, but the catalog text didn't cite the neck's wood species). The fretboard had acquired a fourth dot.

What's interesting about the Round-Up that Mike played as a child and the Round-Up presented to him by Steve Evans in 2009 is that they were both made in 1934 and may have been made in the same production run—Evans had studied production information stamped inside the sound hole of his instrument.

Evans: "There are a couple of identifying features seen in the picture on the cover of Mike's book. His dad's guitar had four position dots instead of three as used on the previous year model. And his dad's guitar had twelve frets clear of the body, instead of fourteen as seen on the Round-Up the following year. I also saw that his

dad had added a trapeze tailpiece, probably in attempt to get the string height lower."

Steve also detailed the chronology of the Gene Autry series of cowboy guitars: "I think the Round-Up is rare, but it's not expensive when you find one. Sears sold that same Round-Up scene on a traditional wooden acoustic guitar for more than twenty years—the Round-Up from 1932 to 1938, the Melody Ranch from 1941 to 1955, and Silvertone— with no Gene Autry signature—from 1958 to 1959.

"So, there were a bunch of Gene Autry guitars made, but the Round-Up is the rarest version, and it would be extremely difficult to find another fall of 1934 model.

"I always said that if I could only own just one cowboy guitar, it would be a Gene Autry. Gene was the original singing cowboy, and his namesake guitar was the first of its kind too. When I decided to retire and I sold the guitars in my guitar museum in 2020, the one cowboy guitar I kept was a 1932 Gene Autry Round-Up.

"Actually, I would have kept more, but my wife had told me, 'Don't bring anything home when you retire.'"

15

1966 PENNCREST-BY-KAY MODEL 1580

It's fair to say that Chicago *used* to be to the guitar manufacturing business what Detroit *used* to be to the automobile industry. The gargantuan Harmony company dominated the budget instrument marketplace for decades, but another Windy City manufacturer, Kay, made Mike Huckabee's Penncrest guitar and amplifier. Like Harmony, Kay also cranked out cheap, no-frills instruments and amplifiers in huge quantities.

In addition to J.C. Penney's Penncrest line, other house brands built by manufacturers in Chicago included Airline (Montgomery Ward), Silvertone (Sears), Old Kraftsman (Spiegel) Custom Kraft (St. Louis Music—wholesale distributor), and dozens more.

Mike's Penncrest model 1580 epitomizes such instruments of that era. It was displayed in the 1966 Penney's Christmas catalog alongside a single-pickup 0905 model, which had a different and more common body silhouette. The 0905—also Kay-made—was priced at $34.50, and the 1580 offered two pickups and a vibrato tailpiece for twenty bucks more. The catalog text did an appropriate job in pointing out the 1580's features and specifications:

"DOUBLE MAGNETIC PICK-UP. Solid-body electric guitar with vibrato tailpiece. New head has 6 keys on one side for easy tuning. Adjustable bridge. Oval rosewood fingerboard with 5 inlaid markers. Selector switch allows units to be played separately or together. Body of maple veneer over hardwood with popular cherry-sunburst finish. Includes instruction book and record, strap and pick."

The four knobs were standard volume and tone controls for each pickup. The handle that manipulated the crude vibrato system is long gone, as is often the case for budget/beginners' instruments.

The vintage guitar phenomenon has its share of whimsical nicknames and phrases, and the slightly over-

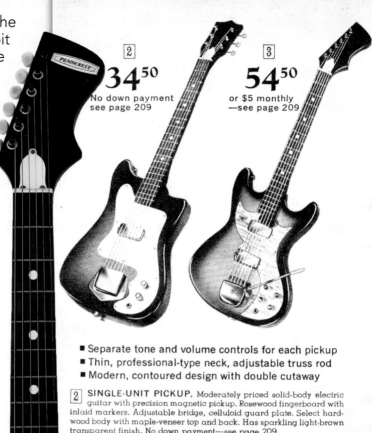

■ Separate tone and volume controls for each pickup
■ Thin, professional-type neck, adjustable truss rod
■ Modern, contoured design with double cutaway

[2] **SINGLE-UNIT PICKUP.** Moderately priced solid-body electric guitar with precision magnetic pickup. Rosewood fingerboard with inlaid markers. Adjustable bridge, celluloid guard plate. Select hardwood body with maple-veneer top and back. Has sparkling light-brown transparent finish. No down payment—see page 209.
X 857-0905 A—Shipping weight 11 lbs.*................ 34.50
X 857-0939 A—Case for above guitar. Wt. 5 lbs.*........ 9.50

[3] **DOUBLE MAGNETIC PICKUP.** Solid-body electric guitar with vibrato tailpiece. New head has 6 keys on one side for easy tuning. Adjustable bridge. Oval rosewood fingerboard with 5 inlaid markers. Selector switch allows units to be played separately or together. Body of maple veneer over hardwood with popular cherry-sunburst finish. Includes: instruction book and record, strap, and pick.
X 857-1580 A—Shipping weight 12 lbs.*................ 54.50
X 857-1598 A—Case for above guitar. Wt. 5 lbs.*........ 9.95

Above: The Penncrest 1580, right, as seen in the J.C. Penney 1966 Christmas catalog. Courtesy of christmas.musetechnical.com

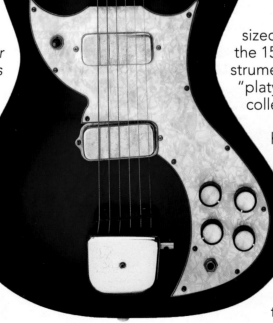

sized headstock silhouette of the 1580 and other Kay-made instruments has been dubbed the "platypus" headstock by some collectors.

As noted earlier, Mike sold his Penncrest guitar and amp to buy a step-up Vox guitar.

But he got the budget duo back, decades later.

"I'd sold those to a gentleman named Norman Gilbey," he recalled. "Fifty dollars for the guitar and the amp. He had children my age, and even as an adult, he thought he'd like to learn to play. I sold them in order to buy that Vox guitar that looked like a Stratocaster; I remember it was in a nice light blue finish. I already had the Clubman bass.

"I pretty much forgot about the Penncrest guitar; I figured it was long gone. Years later—it was probably '98—when I was governor, Capitol Offense was playing the Hope Watermelon Festival. We'd finished our set, and a guy comes up to me and says, 'I don't know if you remember me, but you sold me a guitar.'

"I did indeed remember, and I said, 'Whatever happened to it?' and he said, 'I still have it.' It had been sitting in a closet for about 30 years! He said he had never done much with it because he'd gotten busy doing other things.

"He said, 'Would you like to have it back?' and I said, 'I'd *love* to buy it back!' But he wanted to just *give* it to me; he said, 'It would be an honor to put it back into your hands.' I couldn't argue with him enough to pay for it, so I ended up sending him all kinds of swag from the governor's office. And it was *non-taxpayer-funded* swag; it was stuff to give away that we would purchase privately through a campaign account.

"It was amazing to me that the guitar and the amp were in such great condition. I even got the original guitar stand back; it had been part of the package."

Ultimately, the guitar and amplifier were placed on display in a museum exhibit about Arkansas governors.

VOX CLUBMAN BASS

As of this writing, a sunburst mid-sixties Vox Clubman Bass is the "missing link" in completing the governor's personal wish list of nostalgic instruments, since it was the first bass he ever owned. While the Clubman Bass was inexpensive, a clean example in sunburst has proven to be elusive, so an early '60s catalog illustration of the model—in a solid color—is seen here.

England's Jennings Musical Instruments (JMI) was the parent company of the Vox brand and had been building amplifiers since the late '50s. Electric guitars were introduced circa 1961.

The no-frills Clubman guitar and bass debuted in 1962 as budget instruments. The bass sported 20 frets with a 30-inch scale on a sycamore neck. The thin, laminated body was 15/16 inches thick, which meant that the jack had to be installed on the edge rather than the top. Controls included two volume controls and a master tone knob. Clubman instruments were advertised as being available in red or white finishes.

By the mid-'60s, the Clubman Bass had evolved to a thicker-bodied version, which allowed the jack to be installed on the top (between the control knobs). Sunburst finishes were also seen on some instruments. Huckabee's childhood instrument conformed to this configuration.

Circa 1966, the Oliviero Pigini company (makers of Eko instruments) of Recanati, Italy, began manufacturing Vox guitars and basses. Italian-made Vox instruments were made primarily for the US market, as British production had not been able to keep up with US demand.

CLUBMAN BASS

A low priced fine quality bass guitar with natural polished hardwood reinforced neck. Fitted with Vox bass pick-ups for maximum low frequency response. Finished in red or white fine cellulose. Separate tone and volume controls.

1963 Vox Clubman Bass catalog illustration. Courtesy of Steve Brown/Vintaxe

However, the Clubman Bass was phased out around the time of the transition and didn't make the boat ride from England to the Mediterranean nor the boat ride from the Mediterranean to America. UK Vox guitar production continued through most of the '60s, but those instruments were sold mostly in England and rarely came across the Atlantic after Italian-made Vox instruments appeared Stateside.

YAMAHA FG-180, LATE '60S

Mike purchased this initially-perceived-as-nondescript acoustic guitar simply because he still wanted to have an inexpensive guitar around the house to play, even though he had sold his instruments a few years earlier. He liked the way it sounded, but its construction is a bit more impressive than an initial casual perusal might note.

"I bought that in a pawn shop in Little Rock in 1980," said Huckabee, "and the story on it was that a guy had to hock it to pay a speeding ticket. At the time, I was actually looking for some camera equipment, and I didn't have any guitars at all. When the pawn shop owner told me how much he wanted for it, I thought it would be nice to have just to strum because it played nicely. I told myself, 'At least I'll have something to play.' It was a cheap price, and I could afford it, but that guitar wasn't cheaply made; Yamaha makes decent instruments. It was the only guitar I had for about a decade-and-a-half.

"But that was the first instrument that got me to start up and maintain my interest in guitars once again. At that time, I'd just become pastor of a church in Pine Bluff, Arkansas, and I used it to play for small group meetings or at children's camps."

The dreadnaught-style Yamaha FG-180 was originally made in Japan beginning in 1966. Its manufacturer's suggested retail price was $130 (US). In November 1971, production was shifted to Taiwan, and the model was discontinued in 1974.

The construction and woods of this guitar are noteworthy. The top is made of book-matched spruce, and the sides and three-piece back are mahogany. The neck is made from nato, and the fingerboard is Indian rosewood. The top edge and sound hole feature multiple binding.

Accordingly, this is a better-grade instrument than an observer might initially think.

However, it's also important to Huckabee as a reminder of times past, which is why he's kept it for over forty years.

"It was my first 'small step' back towards guitars," he said succinctly.

1968 FENDER JAZZ BASS

Introduced in 1960, the two-pickup Fender Jazz Bass proffered several new innovative features, making it a logical step-up from the company's original Precision Bass, which had one pickup.

As for its ergonomics, the Jazz Bass had a slimmer neck that was 1 1/2 inches wide at the nut, as well as an offset body style; the waist indentations of the body weren't parallel, as seen on the silhouette of the Precision Bass. The offset recesses on the Jazz Bass made it more comfortable to play when a bassist was seated.

Its two pickups were originally controlled by two concentric volume/tone knobs, but the array soon changed to a two-volume-knob and master-tone-knob configuration. There was no pickup toggle switch on the Jazz Bass.

And this white Jazz Bass is the pawn shop prize that regenerated Mike's interest in basses. While it is a fine utility instrument and is historically important to Huckabee, it has some incongruities that most informed guitar aficionados would notice.

"Janet found that in a pawn shop right after I became governor, in the late summer of '96," said Huckabee. "She knew I was looking for a bass, and I hadn't had one since I sold all my gear. She also remembered that the one I'd had was a Fender Jazz Bass but a different color. She called me and described it, and when she told me the price, I told her to buy it. So, for me, it was 'sight unseen.'

"That instrument kind of got me back into 'the bass business.' I used it with Capitol Offense and also with the praise band I joined at Mark Evans' start-up church."

This Jazz Bass does indeed conform to the style of late '60s and early '70s version, as validated by its block markers, neck binding, and black Fender logo on the headstock.

While it might have been—and still might be—a decent workhorse instrument for Huckabee, this bass's value in the world of guitar collecting would most likely be reduced due to a refinish of the body in white (apparently done some years ago, as the finish exhibits some checking). It also has replacement control knobs. Original paint and original parts figure into the collectability and value of classic guitars and basses.

The bass is also missing its handrest pickup cover and bridge pickup cover, which is a frequent occurrence with this model. The bridge pickup cover is known as the "ashtray" in guitar parlance because that's how many Jazz Bass bridge pickup covers ended up being used onstage.

The body refin does appear to have been done by a professional, and the different-style knobs that were installed are unobtrusive and easy to manipulate.

Not long after he acquired the white Jazz Bass, Mike purchased a new Fender Precision Bass Lyte Deluxe instrument (see Chapter Six, "Etc."). It had modern and more versatile features, and he thought it would make a good frontline utility instrument.

But the white Fender Jazz Bass that Janet found was the bass that got Mike started again.

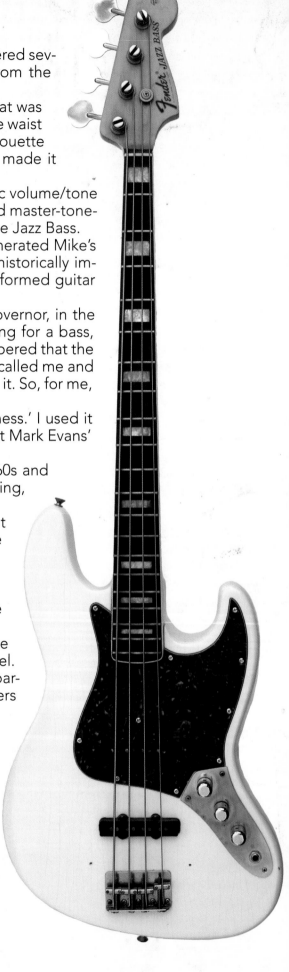

1964 GRETSCH 6119 CHET ATKINS TENNESSEAN

While Mike would ultimately purchase more than one Fender Jazz Bass that reminded him of his previous instrument, those basses weren't *exactly* like the one he had owned before he had to sell all his gear in the '70s.

The same couldn't be said for the Gretsch guitar in his collection, however. Huckabee coveted a model 6119 Chet Atkins Tennessean like the one he used to own, which was also the model played by George Harrison in the Beatles' first movie, *Help!* (although Harrison used other Gretsch guitars in the '60s and beyond).

And Mike found the ideal instrument at Jacksonville Guitars, some six-and-a-half years before store owner Steve Evans gave Mike the 1934 Supertone Gene Autry cowboy guitar cited earlier.

"Mike found me on March 24, 2003," Evans recalled. "He had heard from a musician friend that a guitar like he had been searching for was in my guitar museum. It was a 1964 Gretsch Chet Atkins Tennessean, identical to the one George Harrison played.

"This wasn't a guitar I was planning to sell, but when an Arkansas governor comes into your store with a great story of why he was looking for this particular Gretsch, you bet I was going to let it go to a new home. This was the first time I met Mike."

Many original Gretsch guitars from the '50s and '60s are incongruous—a particular instrument may have slipped out of the factory with a different part or parts on it, compared to what the standard configuration in a catalog might illustrate. Such oddities occupy one of the intriguing facets of Gretsch's history.

However, Huckabee's Tennessean appears to fully conform to the style purveyed by the company (and displayed by Harrison) in the mid-'60s. From the top down, its plain headstock indicates it's probably an early '64 example—a small

Steve Evans and Governor Huckabee with the 1964 Gretsch Chet Atkins Tennessean that Huckabee purchased. Photo by Bob Tanner, courtesy of Steve Evans.

chrome nameplate was added during that annum, but it's not on this one.

It also sports Van Ghent tuners, a zero fret, and neoclassic fret markers (Gretsch aficionados have dubbed such markers "thumbprints") on a rosewood fingerboard.

The finish of the single-cutaway "Electrotone" body (1 7/8 inches deep) was called dark cherry red in a Gretsch ad, and the faux f-holes were painted onto the top.

The two Hi-Lo 'Tron pickups controls included separate volume knobs on the lower bout and a master volume knob on the treble cutaway. Toggle switches on the upper bout controlled pickup selection and tone, and the toggle switch on the lower bout was a standby switch.

The straight bar bridge and the vibrato system were made by Bigsby (and the V-shaped cutout was exclusive to the Gretsch brand).

It goes without saying that Mike is particularly gratified to have acquired this particular guitar, since it not only references his prior ownership of a similar instrument, but it also reinforces his Beatles fixation, then and now.

2008 FENDER '70S JAZZ BASS

Around a decade after the new millennium began, Mike went personal in a big way with his growing collection when he contacted a Fender representative and ordered a reissue of a Jazz Bass that looked like the one he had owned in his younger years. Fender's name for the retro model was '70s Jazz Bass. It had the bullet truss rod system that Fender had introduced on the Jazz Bass, circa 1973, but otherwise resembled Mike's long-gone instrument. His new Fender reissue bass was made in December 2008.

To add to the authenticity, the Fender representative supplied Mike with a set of pickup covers (handrest and "ashtray") and a thumbrest. The parts were installed by Steve Evans.

"I pulled out my 1970 Fender catalog," Evans remembered, "and showed Mike how the thumbrest was originally placed as if you were going to play with your thumb, resting your other fingers on it. He told me to do it like that. He originally said he wanted a white pickguard instead of the black guard this bass came with but changed his mind and decided on a tortoiseshell look. I ordered a USA Fender tortoiseshell pickguard and was pleased when it came in because all the screw holes lined up perfectly. I did, however, have to drill holes to mount the cover plates and the thumbrest, and I was really pleased with how the bass turned out. It looked pretty classy."

And Huckabee averred that he ordered the new bass for stereotypical Baby Boomer time warp reasons. He also commented on the marketing of new expensive guitars in contemporary times.

"I didn't buy it to play," he said. "I bought it for display, purely for the nostalgia value of it. A lot of the stuff I've wanted is the stuff I couldn't afford when I was a kid. I've told manufacturers, 'You guys are trying to sell to eighteen to twenty-year-olds. If you're trying to market your high-end guitars to that age group, they can't buy 'em because they haven't got any money! You need to market your high-end guitars to people my age because we've finally gotten to the place where we can afford them.'"

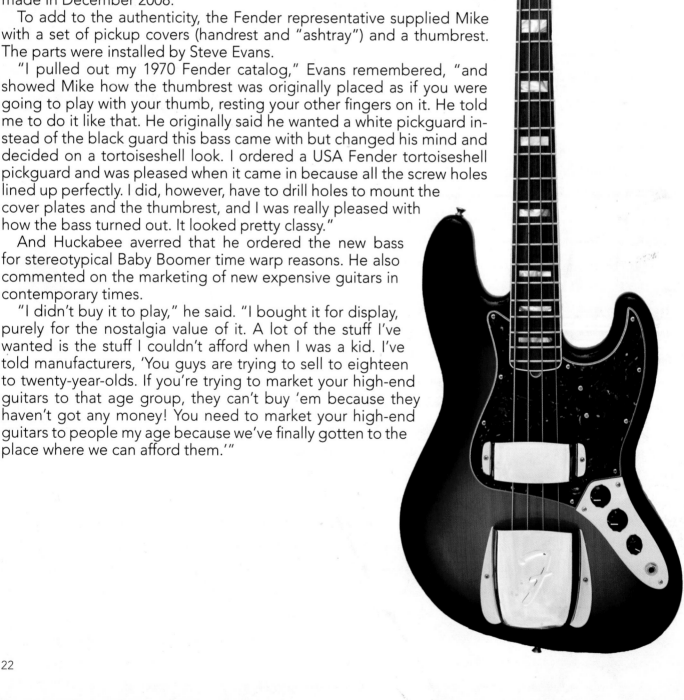

1962 FENDER JAZZ BASS

The most valuable instrument in Huckabee's collection—at least, in terms of dollar value—is his 1962 Fender Jazz Bass. It happens to be a pre-CBS instrument—the Fender company was sold to CBS in early 1965.

The unbound neck and dot fretboard markers on Mike's bass also confirm its early '60s pedigree. Mike acquired this bass after he had already gotten his '70s Jazz Bass reissue.

"I bought that several years ago from a family in New York," he recalled. "The father had bought it new, and he played it in clubs and churches; it still had the original case. He had passed away, and they had read about how I was trying to find gear that matched the stuff I'd had to sell when I was at Southwestern.

"They got in touch with me through my website and told me they were liquidating his estate. They said he would have been thrilled if it ended up with someone who appreciated the instrument. Their dad had watched me on TV and would have loved for me to have this bass. Was I interested in buying it?

"We communicated back and forth; the family sent pictures and validated that it was a 1962 [model]. I'd been looking for something like this for years—I'd still hit pawn shops, and I had people on the lookout for instruments. Occasionally I'd find one from that era, but usually they were from later years and they were *crazy* expensive. We're talking sell-a-kidney prices. I was never going to pay that much for one.

"The family had done enough research to know it was a valuable instrument, and I got it for a price that was fair for them and for me. It's actually older than the one I'd had to sell."

3. SOUVENIRS WITH STRINGS

One interesting facet of Mike Huckabee's collection is the disproportionate number of basses and guitars that were given to him outright. He's been a popular speaker at conventions, business seminars, Christian institutions, and nonprofit organizations for decades, and on many occasions, his appearance has included the presentation of a complimentary stringed instrument.

Regardless of the type of bass or guitar and/or its desirability and/or value and/or whether it's American-made or imported, Mike's always appreciative of such a gesture, as it makes his memory hearken back yet again to the tough times in Fort Worth and how his reversal of fortune now meant that fans of his were actually gifting him with instruments. He's bemused by and grateful for such unexpected and personal benevolence.

"It's a little overwhelming," he admitted, "because it usually happens at a large event, and it's not like you're getting a T-shirt or a ball cap or a plaque. When someone gives you something that you're fond of, it's cool because there's that personal connection. When someone says, 'I made this guitar and I want you to have it,' it becomes very special. The same thing applies to guitars that some group or organization has had especially made for me, like my Muckelroy bass. It's not some standard factory-made Gibson or Fender.

"And I would never sell any instrument that was made specifically for me, whether I ordered it from a builder or if it had been built or ordered for me by someone else and was presented to me as a surprise."

It almost goes without saying that guitar companies have also presented Huckabee with guitars and basses, hoping that the instruments will show up on his show.

BREEDLOVE B22 ACOUSTIC BASS

This exquisitely crafted instrument is an example of a surprise token of appreciation presented to Mike for speaking to a particular organization or group.

"I spoke to a fundraiser for a pregnancy center in a small town outside of San Antonio [Texas]," he recalled. "This is gorgeous, and it sounds gorgeous."

That said, Huckabee noted that he "almost never" plays acoustic bass on his show.

"I used one a couple of times on the Fox show," he recalled, "when I had someone on who was a notable country singer and wanted to do something in an unplugged version. Mostly, I've used those types of instruments at camps with just acoustic instruments around and no PA system."

This bass, completed in January 2010, has a modern body silhouette that is exclusive to the brand. It's a Masterclass variant; all Breedlove instruments in that category are custom-made, using higher-grade woods. They also feature koa binding and an abalone "spoked" rosette around the sound hole.

The neck is made of maple and is 1 3/4 inches wide at the bone nut. Scale is thirty-four inches. The fretboard, pinless "winged" bridge, and headstock overlay are ebony. The top is book-matched bearclaw Sitka spruce (so named due to the mild, naturally-occurring striations in the wood pattern) and the back and sides are myrtlewood.

The trim includes "Life Is Precious" phrase inlaid in script on the eleventh and twelfth frets. The truss rod cover on the headstock is wood and has "Huck" etched into it.

The bass was constructed using Breedlove's own bracing system with a bridge truss designed by JLD Guitar Research and Development for extra support. It has an LR Baggs "Element" active electronics system.

There are two signature signatures on the label inside the sound hole—Kim Breedlove ("Master Luthier, Artist") and Jayson Bowerman ("Master Luthier").

BUCK OWENS ACOUSTIC GUITAR, 2010

Buck Owens was not only a legendary singer and songwriter, but he was also an astute and successful businessman.

Owens and his band, the Buckaroos, were one of the most iconic combos in music history. They were considered one of the twin pillars of country music's Bakersfield Sound, which evolved in the '50s and '60s (the other pillar being Merle Haggard & the Strangers). The Bakersfield Sound was generally defined as a gritty style of country music with drums for dancing, anchored by the twang of a Fender Telecaster guitar. Its fans tended to be stereotyped, sometimes unfairly, as farm laborers and oil workers.

One of the most popular celebrity-associated guitars ever marketed was the red, white, and blue "Buck Owens American" acoustic guitar (model H169), which was made by the Harmony company of Chicago.

Other manufacturers had also built prototype patriotic instruments for Owens to consider when he began developing the guitar, circa 1969. Jim Shaw, longtime keyboard player for the Buckaroos and operations manager for Buck Owens Productions, recalled that the Mosrite, Fender, and Ovation companies also submitted instruments, but Harmony won the Owens's "audition."

The Harmony guitar featured a "Buck Owens—American" inscription on its headstock, and in addition to standard marketing in the guitar business, it was also featured in the then-formidable Sears-Roebuck catalog.

However, Harmony closed its doors in 1976, the last of the American budget guitar manufacturers to succumb to the onslaught of imported instruments.

The notion of giving away patriotically painted guitars began with Owens and the Harmony-made instruments.

"Buck started that tradition in the early '70s," Shaw said. "He gave away hundreds of them over the years."

The model was later reintroduced twice. Ironically—but perhaps not surprisingly—both versions were imported, and just the name Buck Owens was seen on the headstock. Still, the guitar had an Americana vibe.

"The second series was made in Korea in the late '70s," said Shaw. "Buck worked with the designers and

Huckabee with Buckaroos keyboard player Jim Shaw at the Crystal Palace—Courtesy of Buck Owens Productions

approved the prototype; [Buckaroos steel guitar-ist] Tom Brumley heped. In the early '90s, Buck approved a third series built in the Chinese Fend-er factory."

Owens died in March 2006.

Huckabee received his Buck Owens guitar with a personalized message on the pickguard from Buck Owens Productions on November 30, 2010. The presentation followed his participation in a political campaign event that had been staged at Owens's legendary entertainment complex and restaurant in Bakersfield, the Crystal Palace.

Huckabee jammed with the Buckaroos, and Shaw remembered that the band knew in advance that the Arkansas bass player was going to be sitting in.

"Although sometimes the jam sessions are 'seat of the pants,' this one was set in advance," he said. "[There was] no rehearsal. I remember playing 'Mustang Sally.'"

"They knew going in that I was a huge Buck Owens fan," Mike recalled with a grin. "It was a wonderful event. I loved that place."

This 1971 Sears catalog page featured the Harmony-made Buck Owens "Red, White and Blue American guitar"—courtesy of musetechnical.com

JACK CHASE ACOUSTIC GUITAR

This instrument needs to be viewed vertically to understand the unusual inlay. A close perusal reveals that the fretboard inlay is a baby, in utero, sucking its thumb. The meandering line that runs down the fretboard and apparently into the sound hole represents an umbilical cord.

It was built by Jack Chase of Wichita, Kansas, and was given to Mike following his participation in a fundraiser in that city.

CIGAR BOX BASS MADE BY ROBERT BROWN

Robert Brown gives most of his instruments away. He has no aspirations or pretensions whatsoever about marketing the guitars, basses, and other stringed instruments he builds. Such instruments don't even have a brand name, and he fully acknowledges that he is committed to his primeval/hobbyist luthiery because of the personal satisfaction he gets from creating unique instruments that make music.

Accordingly, this fully functional cigar box bass underlines the eclecticism of Mike's collection, and it also has a family connection in its builder.

"My son's father-in-law drives trucks," said Huckabee, "and once he's done for the day, he often gets into one of his hobbies, which is building guitars. He started with cigar boxes. Now he uses all kinds of items."

Brown worked in the medical field for decades and later attained his Commercial Driver's License (CDL), noting that he is "the type of person that needs to work and wanted to travel."

He experienced a battle with cancer, which generated what he termed "the need to focus on something, which was accomplished when I happened on an article about the concept of Delta Blues and how cigar boxes, broom handles, and a wire created a portable music rhythm to the songs sung. So, I made an instrument, then another and another.

"I have been creating instruments for at least ten years. All of my instruments are individually handcrafted from scratch by me; no two are the same. I get an idea, start collecting parts, and start building. Problems occur, and the design changes. When I'm finished, it's usually not what I had in mind but better.

"The hardwood is from the lumberyard store, off the shelf. I whittle, scrape, and sand by hand. The tuning keys and fretwire are from a music store. The electronics are purchased individually, but I normally do the soldering and installation.

"I don't make them to sell, as that would take the fun out of it. However, when I'm finished with an instrument, I usually have no problem with someone wanting to buy it, so [the instruments] sell themselves. Or I give them away as presents."

Brown noted that he prefers to go at his own pace, and special orders aren't particularly encouraged.

"When I did build one on assignment, there was more pressure than fun," he explained, "so I try to avoid that."

"I admire the fact that he's so clever," said Huckabee." He doesn't make the same thing twice! He's made banjos, which is not an easy thing to do. The cigar box bass is fairly recent; I got it around 2015."

The headstock on this bass validates Brown's no-frills approach. The nut is a bolt with the head cut off, and string guides are simple wood screws.

Now in retirement age but still actively making instruments, Robert Brown has a pragmatic attitude about each instrument he builds.

"The one I built in my shop for Mike several years ago was a Christmas gift," Brown detailed. "It was all done by hand, and I could not tell you what pickups I used. However, I can say that I tend to view every [instrument] I build as my last one, so I try to use the best parts that are available."

There are probably thousands of other casual/hobbyist builders like Robert Brown who take pride in the instruments they've crafted, even if they're not particularly trying to sell them.

And by the way, Nicaragua's Brick House cigars have been ranked high internationally among brands.

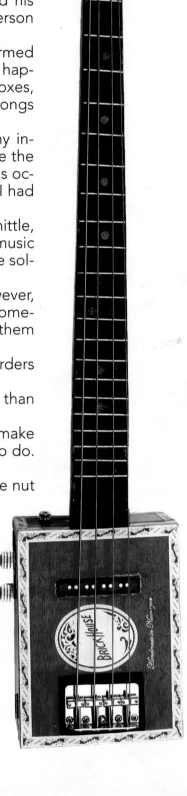

CUPIT TRAVEL GUITAR

One might expect a travel guitar to have a somewhat unusual configuration due to size/space considerations, but the Cupit travel guitar has one of the most bizarre designs ever seen, for a guitar of *any* size. The instrument was introduced at the Summer NAMM in 2011 by veteran Nashville producer/songwriter/author/inventor Jerry Cupit, who later founded an organization called Guitars for Soldiers to distribute some of his downsized musical instruments to military personnel on deployment.

Mike was given this example at a later Summer NAMM.

Jerry Cupit had moved from Louisiana to Nashville in 1980. He worked his way into more than one facet of the music business, ultimately founding the Cupit Music Group, which operated a recording studio, record label, and publishing business.

He wasn't a luthier, but he also had a knack for envisioning unique musical instruments. The idea for a travel guitar germinated around 2007, according to Dan Hagar, who was a consultant/project manager for Cupit's unique instrument.

"He was an outside-the-box thinker and was always coming up with fascinating ideas," said Hagar. "He was determined to make a travel guitar that could be carried on a plane, bus, or car without taking up the space of a full-size acoustic guitar.

"He also wanted this travel guitar to be able to fit into his saddlebags on his Harley Road King [motorcycle] while he and his wife were out on trips," Hagar added with a chuckle.

Numerous prototypes were created, as the size of the guitar was methodically reduced. The final design weighed four pounds.

The compact instrument had a spruce top and dark stained mahogany body, which had a depth of three inches. The round hole on the front came first, according to Hagar:

"It had to have a main sound hole like all acoustic guitars. We later added three small-diameter holes on the top edge of the guitar that faces the player. This opened up the sound greatly and also worked as a personal monitor system for anyone that played it. We also added one f-style hole on the front, above the main sound hole. This seemed to help brighten up the guitar, eliminating it from sounding boxy."

The fingerboard has 17 frets, with truncation beginning on the 12th fret. This practical design means that a player can still get to high notes on higher-tuned strings.

"This guitar could be tuned to standard 440," Hagar detailed, "but due to its size, we always recommended tuning it up to A, which had the best overall sound. It was much like putting a capo on the fifth fret of a full-size guitar."

Placing a piezo pickup under the bridge was an aftermarket option, and the company received a photo from Germany that showed a customer playing an electrified version of the diminutive instrument through a large (and loud) Marshall amplifier stack.

The 2013 Guitars for Soldiers initiative (one sponsor guitar matched by the Cupit company with a second guitar) was an ideal concept for the minimal size of the Cupit. The program continued, overseen by Hagar, while Jerry was undergoing treatments for bone cancer.

Sadly, the Cupit guitar's time in the travel guitar market was relatively short-lived. Jerry Cupit died in 2014 at the age of sixty, and of this writing the Cupit travel guitar is no longer being produced.

"Jerry had a designer patent, an inventor patent, and a utility patent on that guitar," said Hagar. "After his passing, his wife kept all the patents and trademarks updated. It's lying dormant for the time being, but there have been some discussions of a possible relaunch."

DANELECTRO DANO 63 BASS

The most popular American-made guitars of the '60s guitar boom were the Silvertone "amp-in-the-case" models, which were made, like Mike's solid-state Silvertone bass amplifier, by New Jersey's Danelectro company.

The Silvertone amp-in-the-case guitars had bodies made from poplar and Masonite, with one or two pickups that were housed inside lipstick tube casings, as was the construction style of other Danelectro-made guitars and basses in the mid-'60s.

While Danelectro made their own brand of guitars and amplifiers, as well as a few rare instruments that were house brands other than Silvertone, Sears's amp-in-the-case guitars ruled the budget instrument roost in that era.

"I had one of those," recalled veteran rock guitarist Jon Butcher, "Who *didn't*?"

However, the '60s guitar boom was so huge that American budget guitar manufacturers were unable to keep up with the demand, which led to a huge influx of imported instruments. Several domestic builders—including Danelectro, Kay, and Valco—ceased production before the decade was out. As noted previously, Harmony lurched along until 1976.

California's Evets Corporation revived the Danelectro name in a big way in the mid-1990s, and many of their creations were modern instruments that were influenced by the originals, including models that were exclusive to Sears.

Steve Ridinger, president of the Evets Corporation, hosted a political fundraiser for Huckabee during the 2008 presidential campaign, where he presented Mike with the bass shown here.

Known as the Dano 63 model, its body has a slightly different construction style (plywood frame instead of poplar frame, pressed wood front and back instead of Masonite). Its lipstick tube pickups conform to the original style. It has an improved and intonatable bridge, and better-grade tuners, compared to the '60s originals. The neck is maple with a rosewood fingerboard.

And it also has a full 34-inch scale, which Silvertone basses didn't have, with one exception. Throughout Danelectro's relationship with Sears, Silvertone basses had short scales, except for one full-scale solid-body style made shortly before the New Jersey manufacturer closed. For that matter, the body style of the Dano 63 bass was only seen on Silvertone amp-in-the-case guitars; there was no matching bass (even short scale) with this silhouette.

The Dano 63 has a hodge-podge design that still has a vintage vibe, and the present-day Danelectro company has continued to make and market plenty of other multi-influenced/ inspired-by guitars and basses that give a tip of the headstock to their progenitors from the '50s and '60s.

"My first guitar was from Penney's," Mike commented, "but it could just as easily have been from Sears. When I was growing up, the closest music store was in Texarkana, and those instruments seemed to be too expensive for most people, so we just ordered our gear from catalogs."

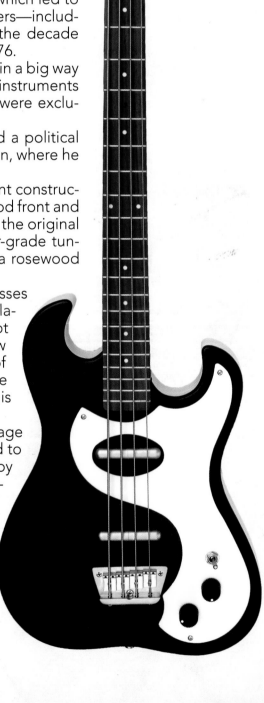

DEAN EDGE BASS, 2012

Like other corporate officials of instrument companies, a Dean company officer saw Mike playing bass on television.

"He got in touch with me," Mike recalled, "and said, 'Y'know, you ought to have a Dean in your inventory.' He had no illusions about me playing it all the time. The one he gave me plays well and has a neck that's really smooth."

The bass presented to Mike is a 2007 Edge Pro Tiger Eye model, now discontinued. Its neck is indeed smooth because the bass has neck-through construction, with a maple center section, basswood sides, and a flame maple top in a "Tiger Eye" finish. The fretboard is rosewood and has 24 frets; the scale is a standard 34 inches.

The nut is brass (which enhances the strings' resonance) and is 1 1/2 inches wide at the headstock juncture. The instrument features gold tuners, knobs, and unique "Monolithic Quick Change" individual bridges for each string.

Electronics include two active pickups. The upper two controls are for volume and pan/blend, and the lower knobs are treble, midrange, and bass tone controls. Such a control array has become popular on instruments with active circuitry.

EPIPHONE EL SEGUNDO ACOUSTIC BASS, 2001

The Epiphone guitar company was purchased by the Gibson guitar company in 1957. Gibson-made guitars bearing the Epiphone moniker were made in the same factory as Gibsons, to the same quality standards, and were marketed by retailers who did not have a Gibson franchise.

In 1970, Epiphone production was switched to overseas manufacturers, and in more recent times, the brand has been proffered as a starter/student/budget line.

"I'd bought the El Capitan [acoustic bass]," said Huckabee (see Chapter Six, "Etc."), "and then Gibson gave me the El Segundo."

A decent entrant into the world of unplugged music, this El Segundo is a full-scale acoustic bass that has a set maple neck with a rosewood fretboard, mahogany body, and laminated maple top (later versions had a select spruce top). The instrument could be run through amplification via a built-in Shadow piezo pickup and an Epiphonic Six preamp.

EPIPHONE FT-112 BARD, CIRCA 2009

The token twelve-string guitar in Huckabee's collection is from a limited-run reissue of Epiphone's FT-117 "Bard" model. It's the make and model that the late Roy Orbison used to craft many of his iconic songs, including "Oh, Pretty Woman" and "Only The Lonely," among others. Orbison's guitar was made in 1962, and the reissue was authorized by his estate. It was designed and built with faithful adherence to the construction of the original, including internal bracing. The body had a solid spruce top, a solid mahogany back, a rosewood bridge, and vintage-style tuners.

The label inside the sound hole matches the light blue label found inside the original, and "Oh Pretty Woman" is stamped on it to designate it as a unique reissue. The song title is also found on the back of the headstock.

There was also a certificate of authenticity signed by Roy's widow Barbara, a pair of sunglasses, sheet music, and other Orbison memorabilia reproductions included with the package.

"The Gibson official who gave it to me said that Roy's widow had wanted me to have it," said Mike. "It happened during a book tour."

EPIPHONE MM-30 MANDOLIN, CIRCA 1999

There's only one mandolin in Mike's collection, so observers might think it's a token instrument, (like the banjo cited in Chapter Six).

"I actually got that one from a publishing company when they published a book of mine called *Character IS the Issue,*" he clarified. "It's pretty common for the author of a new book to receive some kind of gift. This time, the publisher was in Nashville, so they got me a country and bluegrass instrument."

Mike's Epiphone MM-30 dates from the turn of the millennium and is based on a Gibson A-style mandolin. It's been in the Epiphone line in different variations for many years. This particular incarnation has a solid spruce top, mahogany neck and body, and gold hardware. Its scale is 14 inches.

2009 FENDER AMERICAN STANDARD STRATOCASTER

The Fender American Standard Stratocaster is a classic take on a classic model. Introduced in 1954, the Strat (and its copies) became the world's most popular solid-body electric guitar configuration. Its three-pickup versatility and logical innovations have been lauded by professional guitarists in numerous musical genres, and that's still the case today—the model has never been out of production.

"Fender gave me a couple of guitars for promotion on the show," Mike detailed, "and Gibson did, too. The guitars are usually played by musical guests, but sometimes our house musicians will use them."

This example is so clean most guitar enthusiasts would surmise that it's in the New Old Stock (NOS) category, particularly since it still has the sticker on the pickguard that touts its features and benefits.

2009 GIBSON GARY MOORE LES PAUL BFG

This one looks like it belongs to a cast member from *The Road Warrior* or some other movie in the Mad Max series.

But Mike's Gary Moore Les Paul BFG shown here, a gift from Gibson, is fully factory original. Its aesthetics include no markers on the rosewood fretboard, mismatched pickups, mismatched knobs (only three), and a "kill" switch on the upper bout location where a pickup toggle switch would normally be located. The toggle switch on this model is in the location of where a fourth control knob would normally be.

The body has a satin lemonburst finish and the maple top is rough and unsanded; i.e., those stripes aren't just wood grain patterns—they're 3-D.

That said, the Gary Moore Les Paul BFG is fully functional, offering some raucous sounds, in spite of being, er, cosmetically challenged.

IBANEZ TR50 BASS

Here's a personalized New Hampshire-referenced instrument from the 2008 presidential campaign. This Ibanez TR50 bass was custom decorated with a silhouette of the state and presented to Mike.

Ibanez's TR series had debuted in the mid-'90s and proffered a decent, no-frills line of basses. The one-pickup TR50 was the starter model. One unique aesthetic was the installation of the volume control on the pickguard and the tone control on the body.

IBANEZ SOUNDGEAR BASS

"I love the story on this one," said Mike.

"There was a retired master sergeant named Mark Evans in Chicago—same name as the pastor in Little Rock—who wanted to do something for the people who were serving in Iraq and Afghanistan. He saw a TV interview where one of the troops had said, 'I'm from Chicago, and I miss the pizza!' and something clicked. He started an all-volunteer organization, Pizza 4 Patriots, to ship fully cooked then flash frozen pizzas to the troops.

"He went to DHL [shipping] and got them to donate the transportation, then he went to numerous pizza places in the Chicago area, and it went further from there; you could say the organization was based in Chicago.

"I had him on my show, which gave it a good promotion, and he raised a boatload of money to get pizzas over there. He was on the show two or three times. I thought it was just a wonderful, American way thing to show that much appreciation and just give away that much to military personnel halfway around the world. On one of his appearances, he brought that bass; he'd had someone paint the Pizzas 4 Patriots logo on it.

"Mark's now deceased."

JCX GOLDDIGGER BASS

Alabama guitarist Jeff Cook is one notable player who also has decades of experience in designing and playing unique instruments. Many of his guitars and basses were custom-painted by commercial illustrator Wayne Jarrett of Greensboro, North Carolina. Jarrett also specialized in painting motorcycles, drag racers, vans, and automobiles (Think: NASCAR) as well as guitars. In addition to Cook, Jarrett's list of clients has included Jeff Carlisi, founding lead guitarist for 38 Special and Mick Mars of Mötley Crüe.

Moreover, Jarrett painted Mosrite and Gospel guitar bodies for Semie Moseley's company when Mosrite's production facility was located high in the Blue Ridge Mountains in Jonas Ridge, North Carolina during the '80s. Cook had introduced Wayne and Semie at a NAMM show.

And the Alabama guitarist and the artist would ultimately co-own a small business known as Cook-Jarrett Enterprises, marketing the JCX brand of guitars and basses.

"I painted my first guitar for Jeff in '81," Jarrett remembered, "soon after they'd broken through nationally and had left Myrtle Beach behind." (Originally known as Wild Country, Alabama had been the house band at the Bowery, a legendary club in Myrtle Beach, South Carolina, for a number of years.)

Cook would hang out at Jarrett's shop whenever possible, and those visits were the catalyst for their business collaboration.

"Whenever the band took a break, he'd be up here for two or three days," said Jarrett. "I had probably painted a total of 25 to 30 instruments of his when we started the company."

Cook-Jarrett Enterprises was established in the late '80s and was in business for about ten years, according to Jarrett, who recalled that there were no "production" or "stock" instruments made.

"They were all custom instruments," he said, "and the finishes were all different; no two alike. I developed a technique using Saran Wrap, of all things, to create a marble finish. That's what's seen on the bass that was given to Mike Huckabee."

One of the innovations that Cook and Jarrett interpolated was to intermingle parts from more than one classic electric guitar into crafting unique instruments.

"We'd take a Stratocaster-type body and put Telecaster-type parts and electronics on it," Wayne recalled.

Cook and Jarrett both had bigger job priorities than their small guitar company, and the meticulous creation of one-of-a-kind custom guitars and basses meant that JCX instruments would turn out to be rare birds. Jarrett recalled that some forty to fifty instruments were made, of which ten or twelve were basses, and the rest were guitars.

Wayne continued to apply custom finishes to Jeff's personal instruments—before, during, and after Cook-Jarrett Enterprises. The illustrator estimated that, over the decades, he custom-painted approximately 100 instruments for the Alabama guitarist.

"That one was totally unsolicited," Mike said of his acquisition of his JCX Golddigger bass. "Jeff and I got to be friends when Alabama came to the governor's mansion [in 2003]; we also saw each other at NAMM shows. He also had a place in Florida near my residence.

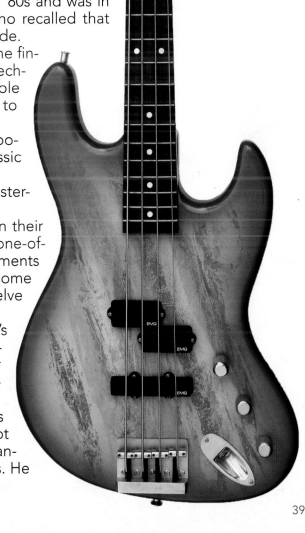

"Jeff had an offshoot band called Jeff Cook & the All-star Goodtime Band, and they played one of the Republican National Conventions. He got me to sit in with his band, and he sat in with my band, Capitol Offense. After the convention, he gave me that bass. Not only is it a beautiful instrument, it plays *really* well."

The design of Huckabee's JCX Golddigger bass (serial #10) validates the policy of Cook and Jarrett to create instruments that draw from more than one classic influence.

The offset body has two active EMG pickups set up in the popular P/J configuration, and the top mounted, angled jack is usually found on a Fender Stratocaster. Most likely, the banana-shaped headstock would be described by guitar lovers as a "reverse Explorer" style, as Gibson's Explorer guitar was the first model from that manufacturer to display

a headstock with that silhouette, albeit right side up. While the tuning keys are mounted on the underside of the headstock, some guitarists and bass players will opine that tuners installed in that location are easier to tune when playing onstage.

The gold hardware is cool too.

2010 KALA U-BASS-FS

A definitive innovative stringed instrument, the U-Bass was introduced in 2009 by Kala Brands. It is, as its moniker implies, a bass ukulele, and its sound is impressive for an instrument its size. It has the same scale length as a baritone ukulele but can actually sound like an upright/"doghouse" bass.

Mike was presented with this example at a NAMM show. When introduced, the U-Bass-FS was considered a top-of-the-line model, according to company representative Ash Reyes Picache. Its body is made from solid mahogany. It has custom Hipshot tuners and a passive Shadow piezo pickup system (there's a jack on its rim for a guitar cord).

The strings are made from a polyurethane blend that the company proclaims as having a "bouncy, rubbery feel." Strings with a more traditional style and feel can also be used. Legendary bassists Bakithi Kumalo and Abraham Laboriel were brought onboard as endorsers, demonstrating U-Bass instruments at NAMM shows and other events.

G.A. LANE "BO DIDDLEY STYLE" BASS

This odd-looking-but-interesting bass exemplifies the extensive handcrafting that many independent luthiers do in the creation of their instruments. Its rectangular body is chambered, with traditional-style f-holes. The interior label, as seen through one of the f-holes, reads: "*Bo Diddley style Electric Bass crafted for Mike Huckabee by G.A. Lane, Fall 2002, Tulsa, Oklahoma. Serial #07.BDB.01*"

"The Bo Diddley shape is basically the theme of the bass—very unusual and unique," Huckabee observed. "I was in Tulsa for a campaign event and was presented with it then."

Other features include a handmade bridge/tailpiece and a Fender P-Bass-style pickup. It has master volume and tone knobs and a three-way toggle switch. Curiously, the pickup beside the bridge/tailpiece appears to be the neck pickup from a Fender Telecaster.

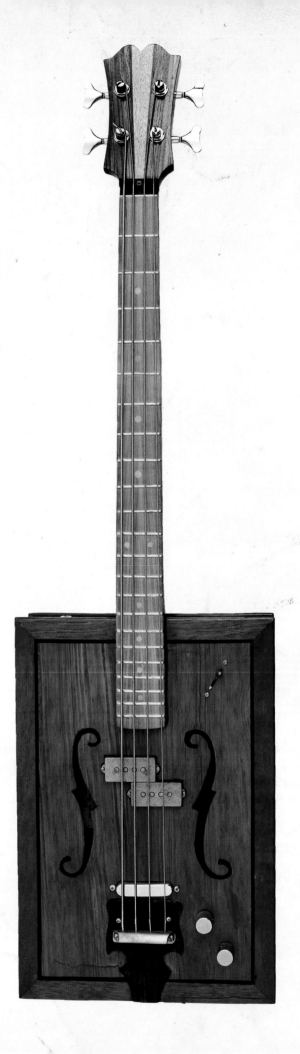

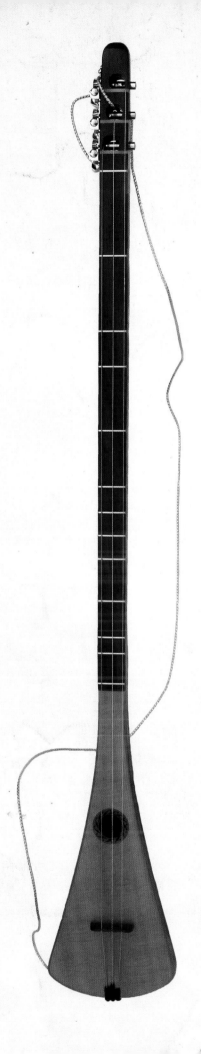

MCNALLY STRUMSTICK

"That was a weird little instrument," Huckabee said with a chuckle, "but it's fun to play. Like the Cupit travel guitar, somebody gave me one at a NAMM show. Essentially, you play the top string, and the other two are harmonic. It's a great gift for people who don't know how to play an instrument. You just basically strum it, and that's the joy of it. You can fret the other strings if you want to, but it was designed so anybody can pick one up and start playing."

The silhouette of the diminutive body of the Strumstick may look slightly familiar to some acoustic guitar fans, as it is similar to the legendary Backpacker travel guitar. Inventor Bob McNally patented that design and later licensed it to the Martin guitar company.

McNally developed the Strumstick as a simpler instrument, tuned diatonically, like a dulcimer. However, it was designed to be played like a guitar. Its three strings are tuned in open G. Its simple design was intended to motivate novice stringed instrument players to continue their personal music education.

MUCKELROY BERNAL BASS

Huckabee received this custom-made, high-quality, multi-laminated bass after speaking to the Texas Music Educators Association (TMEA) in 2012. Its backstory is a quintessential chronicle of American small business success that needs to be detailed.

Luthier Brady Muckelroy founded his business in San Marcos, Texas, in 2011 and began his sojourn by working with his friend Scott Beckwith of Birdsong Guitars. Muckelroy had completed his company's first instrument and was working on instrument #002 and #003 when he was abruptly given an assignment that called for the expedited creation of a custom instrument within several weeks.

"Scott's wife, Jamie Hornbuckle, was the connection for Muckelroy Basses to the TMEA," Muckelroy recounted. "She'd gone to school with that organization's president.

"When the TMEA found out that Mr. Huckabee offered to speak at the convention free of charge, they decided to thank him with a custom bass. Knowing that Jamie was married to a guy who built basses, they call Scott first, but Scott was only building short-scale basses, and Mr. Huckabee preferred a full 34-inch scale bass. So, Scott handed it to me.

"It was an epic challenge. I had less than six weeks to complete the build on top of the vertical learning curve it was to take on. I dug in; I didn't have time to overthink it, knowing I'd probably psych myself out and make an irreversible mistake. I had to jump in feet first with my head on straight, so builds #002 and #003 were put on hold."

Brady's creation was the first example of Muckelroy's top-of-the-line model, the Bernal. The luthier utilized numerous attractive but sonically practical woods with natural finishes.

The neck was three-piece maple, with a curly (flamed) center, and rock maple sides. The slot at its set-in juncture with the body ran all the way to the bridge pickup.

"I ran a deep pocket for maximum sonic transfer from neck to body," Muckelroy explained.

The fretboard is ebony, and there are no markers on its face.

"Only side dots," Brady detailed. "I wanted to leave the fingerboard clean-looking. The mother of pearl side dots have a diameter of two mm."

The body is three-piece (alder core with cherry wings) with padauk stringers. Interestingly, the top of the body and the headstock cap are Macassar ebony, which isn't seen too often as a cap wood.

"Being hands on with many different wood combinations gives me a better understanding of their sonic characteristics," said Brady. "Macassar ebony is a wood used on electric and acoustic instruments alike." "It is very similar to the density and hardness of ebony, but there's some color to the grain. I especially enjoy using it a fingerboard. Tonally—as a top on electric instruments—it gives you a sweeter top end and adds a little focus to the note development. This is especially helpful when lighter or softer woods are used as a body wood topped with Macassar ebony."

The Huckabee bass is a passive instrument. Its electronics feature Kent Armstrong pickups (a Jazz-style in the neck position and a Music Man-style for the bridge). Controls are volume, blend, tone, and a three-way coil switch for the bridge pickup.

The laser-cut TMEA logos on the front and back of the body immediately attract an observer's attention, as does the presentation details on the back. The etchings are the work of Don Evans, also of San Marcos.

"Don also cuts the 'M' logos I use on my headstock," Brady added.

Muckelroy's intense concentration resulted in a beautiful instrument that Mike was delighted to receive.

"My hard work paid off," the luthier said proudly. "The build turned out wonderfully. I got to meet Mr. Huckabee backstage at the convention where he spoke."

"There were some 1,500 professional music educators there from all over the state," Huckabee said of the

Muckelroy Bernal bass, back

Close-up of the TMEA logo on the front of the body

Mike is surprised onstage with the Muckelroy Bernal bass. That's TMEA Executive Director Robert Floyd on the right.—Karen Cross

Backstage with luthier Brady Muckelroy—Karen Cross

2012 event. "[It was] probably one of my better speeches; it was on the value of the arts, and I referred to that program I'd started when I was governor, to get musical instruments to kids. The speech has actually been posted online.

"They presented me with the bass, which was a total surprise. Then I had to sit in with the Texas All-State Jazz band. It's gorgeous, and it plays beautifully. Great action, rich tone. Those kids in the jazz band played great, too."

Some ten years after building the Huckabee bass, Brady Muckelroy reflected on what creating that instrument had done for his fledgling luthiery business.

"The Huckabee bass represents the first domino to tip," he said in 2022. "It was an incredible opportunity for me because I was about a year into building and didn't have any clients—meaning that everything I had built or was building was all on my dime.

"It was the start of some good word of mouth.

It wasn't long after I built that bass that I began getting phone calls with orders. The ball was rolling; momentum had begun. I went from being a nobody in the world of luthierie to being a small blip on the map, and it was that starting point that really set the trajectory for me.

"There is something important that I keep close to my heart at all times: Anything you see coming from me that resembles success is the result of someone else believing in me—giving of their time, their resources, being in my corner, and just flat-out rooting for me. Without these amazing people in my life, my efforts would likely have been short-lived.

"I'm now entering my twelfth year in business with over 500 basses out there in the wild. I have met some incredible people along the way. I love what I do. It lights me up!"

The Muckelroy bass is also a favorite of Huckabee, who noted, "I play this one a lot when I'm practicing in my music room."

OVERTURE HUCK BASS

Another relatively young luthier, Justin Hoffman, had a custom-build experience with Mike that was similar to Brady Muckelroy's story, with one major exception—Mike knew in advance he was going to get the bass and was able to provide input into its design and construction.

Hoffman had started Overture Guitars in East Peoria, Illinois, in 2009. He met Mike at a NAMM show soon after his shop opened for business.

"I told him I was a huge supporter of his television show," Hoffman recounted, "and I wanted to stay in communication with him since I knew he played bass. I asked him if he would be interested in me building a bass for him to play on his show, and he graciously accepted my offer.

"Mr. Huckabee *did* work with me on the bass build. Initially, I sent him a mock-up of the bass and listed the woods I wanted to use. He was satisfied with what I had originally designed. However, when it came to making it his signature instrument, he requested an inlay on the 12th fret that read 'Huck Bass.' We both thought that would fit the bass perfectly. The phrase was laser-etched into the wood and then drop filled with black epoxy."

The Overture bass was built with numerous woods. The top was AAAAA quilted maple with a purpleheart center stripe, and the back was ash.

"I also chose to inlay an abalone stripe down the center of the purpleheart," said Hoffman, "to add an extra wow factor to the signature bass."

The bolt-on neck was a five-piece laminate with curly maple on the sides and a walnut/wenge/walnut center. It had 24 frets on a full 34-inch scale. The fretboard wood was bird's-eye maple.

"I was looking for the resonance and tones that typically come with a hard maple," Justin said of the bird's-eye fingerboard, "but I also wanted to use a wood with character and visual appeal."

Fret markers were abalone. The headstock logo interpolates a cross-and-sword design around the brand name.

The pickup system on the bass included active circuitry for its two Bartolini J-Bass units. The four controls are not volume and tone knobs for each pickup, as might be expected. Instead, they are volume, treble, bass, and blend.

Hoffman recalled that the special build transpired faster than might have been expected.

Right: The rear view of the Huck Bass shows the four-bolt attachment for the neck, the compartments for the controls and battery, and the ferrules where strings load through the body—Courtesy of Overture Guitars

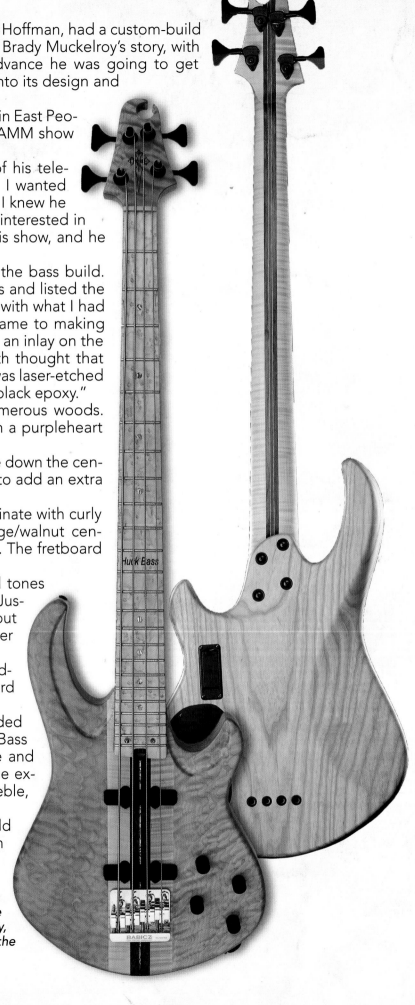

Sporting his recently acquired Overture Huck Bass, Mike hangs out with guitarist Mark Farner on the set of his Fox News Channel television show.—Courtesy of Mike Huckabee

"This custom build went quicker than a traditional build because of the urgency and excitement of who I was building it for," the luthier said. "I communicated with Mr. Huckabee all throughout the build and emailed him pictures of the process; we collaborated together on specifics, especially when it came to the 12th fret inlay with the Huck Bass. I have great respect for Mr. Huckabee, and I wanted to provide him with a product that exceeded his expectations. I shaved off about 40 hours of time building this project, since I put everything else on the back burner and focused strictly on his build until it was complete. A normal bass build usually runs on average around 120 hours. Mike's took around 80-90 hours.

"Mike contacted me once he received the bass and was very thankful and excited to have it. He was extremely satisfied with the craftsmanship and the playability of the instrument."

Sharp-eyed guitar fans may have noticed that the black bridge/tailpiece unit on the bass (seen in the photo with Mark Farner) has been replaced by a gold-plated Babicz aftermarket accessory. The supplantation was facilitated by Jeff Carlisi, who had first met Mike some years earlier at a NAMM show in Anaheim, California, after Carlisi had departed from 38 Special. Jeff and Liberty DeVitto, the erstwhile drummer for Billy Joel's band, had sat in with Mike's band, Capitol Offense.

Later, Jeff approached Mike about writing a foreword for a military book he had been working on with an acquaintance. The musician and the politician discovered they lived, according to Jeff, "about 20 minutes from each other" in the Florida Panhandle.

"We've remained close friends ever since," Jeff said.

Carlisi is also a close friend of bassist John Regan, who is best known for his work with Peter Frampton, and the two veteran players still occasionally work together on musical projects. Regan had a Babicz bridge on more than one of his basses and imparted his enthusiasm for the accessory's intonation and resonance.

Carlisi: "John said that the bridge was amazing and that it had turned his bass into a completely different beast. He told me the company made bridges for guitars, as well, so I was intrigued. He put me in touch with a guy named Jeff Carano, who was a co-owner of the company with Jeff Babicz.

"Jeff Carano explained that they also make bridges for Strats and Teles. I had a 'Franken-Strat' that I also call 'the most expensive cheap Strat in the world,' and they sent me a bridge for that guitar. It dramatically improved the sound."

Carlisi's Babicz bridge was installed by renowned Florida Panhandle luthier/musician Fritz Froeschner.

In a follow-up conversation, Carano, who played bass himself, asked Carlisi if he knew of any bass players that might be interested in Babicz bridges, and Carlisi immediately dropped the name of his neighbor, Huckabee.

"Turns out he's a big fan of the governor," Carlisi said of Carano.

Carano sent a bridge to Huckabee that would be compatible as a replacement on the Overture Huck Bass, and it was installed by Froeschner.

And when Huckabee acquired his highly-collectible 1962 Fender Jazz Bass, Froeschner checked out and set up that instrument.

PERRY GUITAR WITH CHORD BUDDY

While the top of the body of this Perry guitar is attractive, it's probably not surprising that Huckabee was immediately more interested in the gizmo that was attached to the end of the fingerboard (over the first thee frets).

The device with the multicolored buttons is a Chord Buddy, a mechanism that is particularly effective in training and teaching youngsters to develop their musical skills on all types of musical instruments.

"I saw it at a NAMM show," he said, "and was fascinated by it. No surprise there—It's always fun to go to a NAMM show to see and play all of these new, cool things. I brought a company representative onto the television show to try and generate interest among kids who might want to learn to play.

"And I'm all for that, of course."

"JESUS PRAISEWORTHY" CUSTOM TELECASTER COPY

Here's yet another complimentary guitar given to Mike for a speaking engagement, this one at an academy in New Hampshire. It is a copy of an original Fender Custom Telecaster (sunburst body, bound front and rear), made by Mark Reeder. The decals on the headstock read, "Jesus Praiseworthy—The Truth, The Way, The Life—John 3:16."

The engraving on the guitar's neck plate commemorates the event where Huckabee got the instrument.

CREATED BY
MARK A. REEDER
AND PRESENTED TO
MIKE HUCKABEE
ON MAY 30, 2012
ON BEHALF OF
LIBERTY HARBOR
ACADEMY

TOBIAS CLASSIC FIVE-STRING BASS

This is a five-string version of the four-string Tobias Classic model bass Mike has played for years as one of his personal utility instruments on his television show. He recalled that the five-string was presented to him by the Gibson company when production of Tobias instruments cranked up in Conway, Arkansas.

Since the governor has had the four-string Tobias longer and it's one of his go-to basses in Tennessee, the details regarding this brand and model are found in Chapter Seven, "The Hendersonville Utility Trio."

YAMAHA TRB 1005 BASS

In January 2014, an organization called the Percussion Marketing Council hosted a presentation given by Mike, who used the occasion as another opportunity to advocate getting instruments into the hands of youngsters. He was surprised by the PMC with an exquisite Yamaha five-string bass.

Karl Dustman, the PMC's executive director from 2001 to 2020, enthusiastically recalled the event.

"Governor Huckabee has been a constant music advocate for years," Dustman said. "He had addressed the NAMM organization in earlier times during the Anaheim convention in January. I heard him speak both times and knew he could bring a very special element to the PMC membership and general percussion industry's annual meeting.

"Through two or three years of continuous pursuit, we were able to secure his time and appearance for the PMC in January of 2014. This was a significant achievement for the PMC; the governor's schedule was very demanding, as he was preparing to run for president, and these public appearances helped to build his momentum.

"The presentation of a thank you plaque signed by the PMC officers and the presentation of the Yamaha bass guitar with hard shell case was an expression of appreciation for him taking the time and effort to include the PMC annual all-members meeng in his busy itinerary. Knowing of his avid interest in music and playing bass guitar, we thought it appropriate to thank him with a very special bass. We also knew about the sometimes challenging experiences between the drummer and the bass player in most bands. We wanted to embrace the governor as a bass player for appearing at a drummers event."

The short-lived TRB1005 had a body made of figured maple and alder. Its bolt-on neck was also maple, and the fingerboard was rosewood. The instrument had a 34-inch, full scale, and the bridge was solid brass.

The TRB1005's active circuitry proffered a huge sound. The pickups were touted as "Alnico Hum Cancelling" (a reference to the pickup magnets and humbucking wiring), and the controls were arrayed with volume and pan/blend side by side (larger knobs) and three smaller tone equalization knobs. Yamaha's name for this configuration was Q-Mix. Note that the controls still have a thin plastic specifications/instruction card inserted between them.

Interestingly, Huckabee appeared to be playing a borrowed Yamaha TRB1004, the four-string equivalent of the TRB1005, at an Iowa fundraiser in 2010 (see Chapter One, "Bass Quest: A Brief History").

4. SIGNED SOUVENIRS WITH STRINGS

Mike Huckabee is as much of a music fan as anyone, and for years, he has enjoyed collecting instruments that were autographed by some of his favorite players and singers.

"Usually, they have already been signed when they're presented to me," he said of such guitars and basses. "And such presentations have been onstage or at a get-together backstage or elsewhere. If they haven't been signed, I will certainly ask the artist to do that."

Huckabee has even been known to keep a cache of new guitars for guests to sign at the studio from which his TV show is broadcast. Such inventory was stored in New York when he was on Fox News Channel, and he has unsigned guitars at the Huckabee Theater in Hendersonville, Tennessee. A disproportionate number of such instruments are black Behringer budget Stratocaster copies.

Oftentimes, the autographed instrument presented to Mike by someone else is a budget guitar or bass itself, but that's okay—he is still grateful for such additions to the "signed by" category of his collection.

And at one point earlier in his media career, Huckabee oversaw the creation of his own brand of instruments. A signature version of his name appeared on the headstock of the guitars and basses that were marketed, and a large Mike Huckabee logo was emblazoned on the pickguard. The bass fared a bit better cosmetically as it also had "Huckabee" special inlay on the seventh and twelfth frets.

"I had two versions made," he said. "One was a six-string that was kind of a Strat knockoff in sort of a cherry finish, and the Huckabee bass was based on a Fender Jazz Bass—no surprise

Freeze frame: Huckabee shows off his namesake guitar in a promotional video. He also personally autographed this one on the forearm bevel.—Courtesy of Mike Huckabee

there—in red, white, and blue finishes. My son David handled that promotion."

David Huckabee detailed that the instruments were envisioned and built as a type of promotional item for his father's political action committee.

"We used them for a fundraising initiative for Huck PAC," said David, "and we also bought some to give away for charities and auctions. There wasn't a brand per se; they were custom Mike Huckabee signature guitars. The guitar came first, then the bass. We picked a standard guitar and bass, then worked on the signature design. They turned out great."

David estimated that around 100 guitars and 100 basses were made, with approximately 75 percent being sold and 25 percent being donated. Mike would personally sign some of the instruments himself.

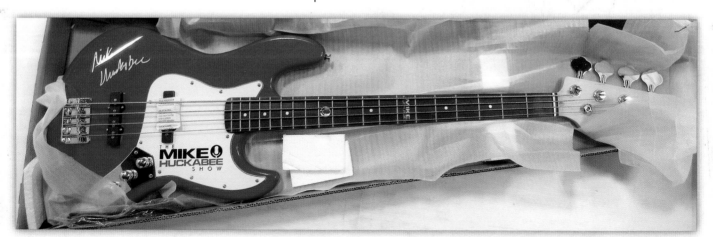

New-old-stock Huckabee bass. It, too, has been manually signed. Note the name of the show on the pickguard and the seventh fret, as well as the microphone logo on the twelfth fret. — Courtesy of Albrecht Auctions

AXL TELECASTER-STYLE GUITAR, SIGNED BY RINGO STARR, AUGUST 22, 2003

"Ringo's All-Starr Band was playing a concert in Little Rock at the Riverfront Amphitheater," Mike recalled, "and David had worked at a radio station when he was in college in Jonesboro. So, he was into all kinds of promotions. I didn't get to go to the Ringo concert, but David decided he would try to get Ringo's autograph; he's one of these guys who can finagle his way into about anything. He got a cheap guitar and managed to get Ringo to sign it to me. The autograph is upside down compared to how most guitars are signed.

"I actually met Ringo and his wife Barbara Bach later, backstage in the green room at the David Letterman show. Clint Black was back there too."

BEHRINGER GUITAR SIGNED BY KRIS ALLEN

Winner of the 2009 *American Idol* competition, Kris Allen—a native of Conway, Arkansas—has known Huckabee for some time and signed one of Mike's Behringer Strat copies.

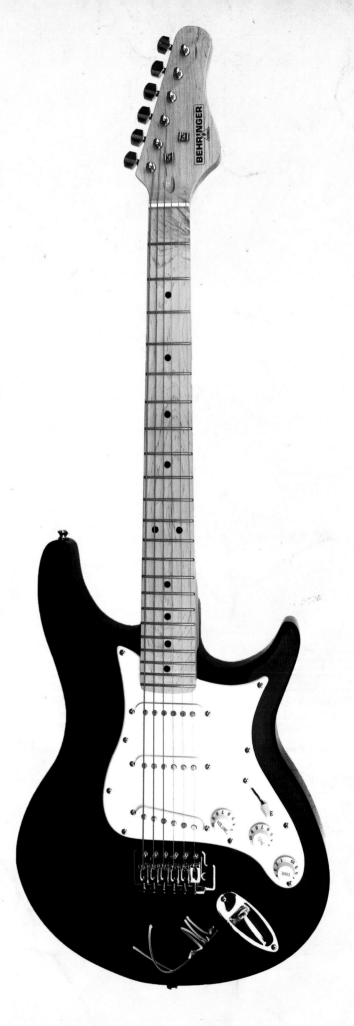

BEHRINGER GUITAR SIGNED BY NEW HAMPSHIRE PRESIDENTIAL CAMPAIGN VOLUNTEERS, 2008

Validating the everyman approach to Huckabee's political campaigns and his guitar collection, this Behringer Stratocaster copy was signed by over 70 workers in New Hampshire during his run for the White House in 2008.

BEHRINGER GUITAR SIGNED BY GEORGE JONES

Country music legend George Jones was a fan of Huckabee's television show, and Mike was a fan of George Jones. "The Possum" appeared on the broadcast in 2009 and later signed a Behringer Strat copy.

When Jones died in early 2013, Mike was called on to eulogize Jones at his funeral at the Grand Ole Opry. Among the other speakers and performers who remembered "The Possum" in words and song were former First Lady Laura Bush, Tennessee governor Bill Haslam, Patty Loveless, Wynonna Judd, Barbara Mandrell, Randy Travis, Charlie Daniels, Vince Gill, Brad Paisley, Alan Jackson, the Oak Ridge Boys, Tanya Tucker, and Kenny Chesney.

"Every time you heard a George Jones song, you knew it was coming from deep inside of him," Huckabee remarked. "He had that quality of being able to sing not just the notes, but to sing the very soul of the song. For decades, he mentored young musicians. His voice is irreplaceable."

BEHRINGER GUITAR SIGNED BY WILLIE NELSON AND RAY PRICE

"They were both on my show on Fox," Mike enthused. "One of the all-time great stories out of Nashville was that Willie Nelson's first job in a band was playing bass for Ray Price, and Willie played the class act with ease; he always remembered the people who helped him on his way up. He was incredibly loyal to Ray Price. Ray had been on my show, and he convinced Willie to come on later. More people ought to know about Ray Price's magnificent voice and how he influenced country music back in the day.

"They actually signed two [guitars]. One was auctioned off for that charity to get musical instruments for kids, and I kept one for myself."

BOULDER CREEK ECL-2, SIGNED BY THE GATLIN BROTHERS AND JAMES DAVISON

While this instrument is the token classical/nylon string guitar in Mike's collection, it obviously doesn't have a classic configuration to its top. There's not only a small sound hole near the neck joint, but the top edge of the rim also features another sound hole as well as a preamp with a built-in tuner.

The top is solid spruce, and the sides and back are rosewood. The unique construction of the instrument has been patented and has what is known as the Suspended Bracing System, which allows more resonance, more projection, and better tone. As is the case on other classical guitars, the fretboard is wider (two inches at the nut). Its scale is 25 5/8 inches.

This example was given to Huckabee by the Gatlin Brothers (Larry, Steve, and Rudy), who signed it when they appeared on his show in New York. He explained the smaller signature near the bridge is that of James Davison, "a businessman from Ruston, Louisiana, who gave the Gatlins a plane ride to New York for their appearance on my Fox show. He's a great guy and somehow got his signature on the guitar!"

Rudy Gatlin recalled that the guitar that the Gatlin Brothers presented to Mike was "one of Larry's guitars that he got several years ago when he first started playing them. Boulder Creek has sent me some [guitars], as I am now on board with the company as well.

"They are fine acoustic guitars; they sound wonderful in the studio and are great road guitars. They have nice electronics and play great. They're easy to tune, and they *stay* in tune."

The Gatlin Brothers have also appeared on Mike's TBN show.

Rudy Gatlin plays a Boulder Creek guitar on Huckabee's show on TBN.—Courtesy TBN

2003 EPIPHONE PROMOTIONAL GUITAR, SIGNED BY ALABAMA

The mega-country band Alabama has had a long-standing positive relationship with Huckabee, and his collection includes three guitars with connections to that musical aggregation, as well as the rare JCX bass he received from that band's lead guitarist, Jeff Cook.

Two of the instruments in the Alabama-Huckabee connection are limited edition Epiphone guitars that the band commissioned in 2003 to mark their twenty-fifth anniversary. The guitars have a Gibson Les Paul Jr. style, but a humbucking pickup powers the sound instead of the usual single-coil P-90-style pickup.

Artwork on the series included illustrations on the top, with a lenticular display of the band appearing (and disappearing) in front of an American flag. The back of the body was imprinted with a chronological list of the band's number-one hits, and the truss rod cover noted the anniversary years.

The unsigned Epiphone Alabama promotional guitar is actually owned by Janet Huckabee, and it's on display here (instead of the previous chapter) to demonstrate the lenticular effect—all the band members are on view in front of the flag on the autographed guitar, but a ghostlike, see-through visage of bassist Teddy Gentry at the lower right of the flag (viewed horizontally) is the only individual seen on the unsigned guitar, thanks to a slight difference in the angle of the camera.

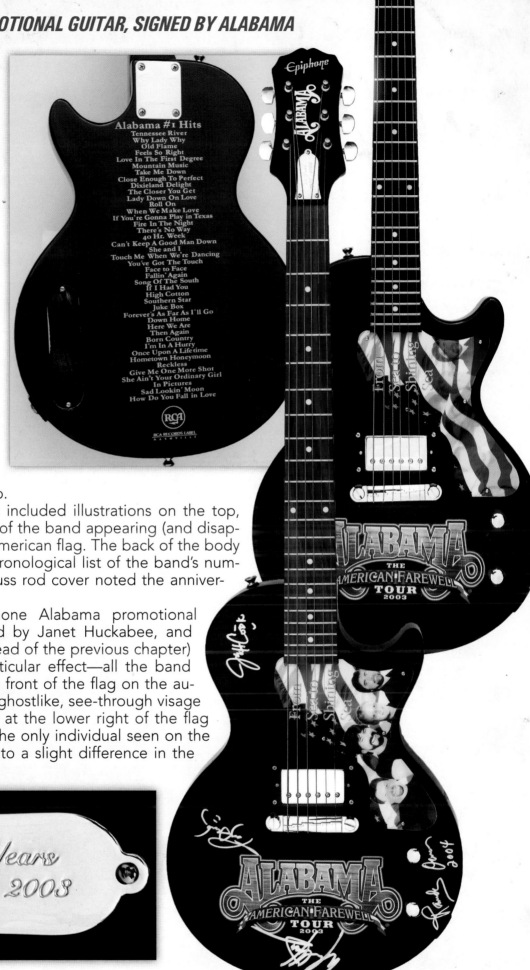

Alabama #1 Hits

Tennessee River
Why Lady Why
Old Flame
Feels So Right
Love In The First Degree
Mountain Music
Take Me Down
Close Enough To Perfect
Dixieland Delight
The Closer You Get
Lady Down On Love
Roll On
When We Make Love
If You're Gonna Play in Texas
Fire In The Night
There's No Way
40 Hr. Week
Can't Keep A Good Man Down
She and I
Touch Me When We're Dancing
You've Got The Touch
Face to Face
Fallin' Again
Song Of The South
If I Had You
High Cotton
Southern Star
Juke Box
Forever's As Far As I'll Go
Down Home
Here We Are
Then Again
Born Country
I'm In A Hurry
Once Upon A Lifetime
Hometown Honeymoon
Reckless
Give Me One More Shot
She Ain't Your Ordinary Girl
In Pictures
Sad Lookin' Moon
How Do You Fall in Love

RCA
RCA RECORDS LABEL
NASHVILLE

25 Years
1978 - 2003

1998 EPIPHONE EB-0 BASS, SIGNED BY COLLIN RAYE

Multiplatinum country artist Collin Raye is a native of De Queen, Arkansas (about 50 miles from Huckabee's hometown of Hope).

"He had a lot of big hits," Mike said of Raye, "and every year, he would come back and do a benefit concert at the football stadium in his hometown of De Queen. When I was governor, I'd always go to what they called 'Collin Raye Day.' It was a big deal, and the money went to local charities. He knew I was a bass player, and he would invite me to come onstage and sit in with his band. That happened several times, and one year he presented me with an Epiphone bass."

The Epiphone EB-0 was a budget variant of its Gibson forebear—short-scale, mahogany neck and body, rosewood fretboard, and a powerful single pickup mounted near the neck joint. However, the Gibson EB-0 had a set-in neck, while the Epiphone version had a bolt-on neck. The three-point combination bridge/tailpiece on the Epiphone was also a more recent innovation.

The inscription on the face of the body reads, *"To Gov. Huckabee, Have fun with this. You're a fine man. It's an honor to know you. Best wishes, Collin Raye."*

FENDER JAMES BURTON SIGNATURE RED PAISLEY FLAMES TELECASTER, SIGNED BY JAMES BURTON, GEORGE JONES, LORRIE MORGAN, AND MIKE HUCKABEE

A huge fan of James Burton, Mike calls the legendary guitarist "one of the nicest, most humble guys you'd ever want to meet. And a lot of people still aren't aware of how important he was in the history of guitar music."

Burton's appearances on *The Adventures of Ozzie and Harriet*, backing up Ricky Nelson, and his lead guitar assignment for Elvis Presley's TCB Band are just part of the historic guitar work he crafted.

A native of Dubberly, Louisiana, Burton is typically associated with a Fender Telecaster. He used a pink Tele with (factory original) paisley decoration during his glory days with Elvis, and his signature instrument was a variant of that model, with a third pickup located between the neck and bridge pickups. Different editions with different features, different finishes, and different paisley patterns were marketed.

Burton was also a fan of Mike's show, and he presented Huckabee with one of the new Red Paisley Flames edition of his signature instrument that had debuted in 2005 at the James Burton International Guitar Festival in Shreveport (and during the same weekend, a statue of Burton was unveiled outside that city's historic municipal auditorium). The '05 version of Burton's guitar had a basswood body, a one-piece maple neck (in a '60s U-shape), and gold hardware. The fretboard has a 9.5-inch radius.

In addition to Burton's signature, the instrument was signed by country stars George Jones and Lorrie Morgan.

"The reason I love James is because he is who he is," said Mike. "There's no pretense at all. And he knows who I am, and we're committed Christians, which is very important to both of us."

Burton uses his signature Telecaster on the Huckabee show.—Courtesy TBN

Mike and Phil Collen jam at a NAMM show. — Courtesy of Mike Huckabee

JACKSON DINKY, SIGNED BY DEF LEPPARD

One of the more unique and enduring relationships that Mike has forged with famous musicians has been his friendship with English guitarist Phil Collen of Def Leppard. In an unexpected and memorable encounter at a NAMM show, Collen and Huckabee conversed briefly and then jammed. They both enjoyed the experience so much they opted to keep in touch.

"Here were two guys who couldn't be more different," Huckabee said, "but we had such a good time."

Ultimately, Collen appeared on Huckabee's show on the Fox News Channel, and the host was presented with a Jackson guitar, signed by Def Leppard.

This Jackson instrument is exemplary of the evolution of electric guitar brands during the '80s (the era of hair bands), with its upside-down "pointy" headstock, sharper beveling on the body edges, and a high-tech vibrato system to allow "dive bomber" sound effects.

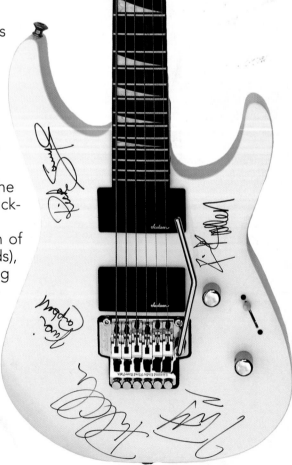

PEAVEY REACTOR, SIGNED BY LYNYRD SKYNYRD

An ancillary "benefit" of instruments that emulate a Fender Telecaster is that the flat front of the body offers a decent area to accommodate autographs, and that's the case for this 1994 Peavey Reactor, an excellent quality American-made utility instrument. It was signed several years after it was built by the members of Lynyrd Skynyrd.

Peavey is headquartered in Meridian, Mississippi, and the company's feisty founder, Hartley Peavey, has lived by his mantra of building "quality equipment for working musicians at fair prices" ever since he started his business in 1965.

What's more, Mike was aware that Peavey had aggressively gone after musicians in the burgeoning Contemporary Christian genre in the '80s, supplying instruments, amplifiers, and sound reinforcement gear to artists such as Mylon LeFevre, White Heart, Petra, and others.

And how many churches have ever relied on a Peavey sound system?

"I think Hartley Peavey is a genius," Huckabee said succinctly.

Mike was given the Skynyrd-signed instrument while he was governor and the band was in town for a concert.

"The promoter of the concert said that the band would like to meet me," he said, "and he arranged for us to get together. We had a luncheon for them at the governor's mansion; they're really down-to-earth guys, a lot like me—good ol' boys who were living way beyond the dreams they had as kids. They'd gone much further in music, and I'd done the same thing in politics. We had that in common. All of us realized how blessed we were.

"And in all honesty, we talked mostly about hunting and fishing. I got to show off a bass boat I had at the time."

The Reactor featured a poplar body and maple neck, with 22 frets and a 25 1/2-inch scale. Its nut was made of a Peavey-trademarked material known as Graphlon.

SQUIER MINI, SIGNED BY TED NUGENT

Another rock star said it best: "You don't get 'Ted Lite.'"

As subtle as a steamroller, Michigan native Ted Nugent has been a loud, uncompromising, and often controversial presence in the sociopolitical facet of popular music for decades. Starting with the Amboy Dukes and their solitary hit "Journey to the Center of the Mind" in 1967, Nugent has been sonically bludgeoning the opposition incessantly for decades, and his usual weapon of choice has been a Gibson Byrdland thinline electric guitar. It's almost like Da Nuge is hunkered down in his own musical foxhole (armed with who knows what kind of firepower), daring anyone to try to jump in with him.

And Huckabee is a fan.

Squier is Fender's budget line. Despite being perceived as a beginner's instrument, this Squier Mini just might provide some unique tonal opportunities to some players because it has a short 21-inch scale, and it's a hardtail (no vibrato). Nugent signed it when he appeared on Mike's show.

SQUIER STRAT, SIGNED BY ALABAMA

Alabama also presented Huckabee with another autographed guitar, this one a 2003 Squier Strat by Fender, at an event at the governor's mansion in Little Rock when the band was in town for a concert. Perhaps not unexpectedly, the governor was called up to the stage to sit in with the band at the show.

SQUIER STRAT SIGNED BY JOSH TURNER

The Huckabee family has a close relationship with the family of singer Josh Turner.

"He's based out of Nashville," Huckabee detailed, "and he's had several number-one hits. I've been friends with Josh since 2008, when we got a campaign contribution from him, and then he endorsed me [for president]. His family came down to our place in Florida, and they also went to Disney World with us once. They also went to the Mediterranean on one of the tours that I sponsored."

WILSON BROS. VMB-75 BASS

The Ventures played numerous brands of guitars and basses during their long history and were best known among their fans for a brief association with Mosrite guitars in the mid-'60s. They had endorsed *and invested* in Mosrite, and the brand's worldwide distribution headquarters was next door to the Ventures International Fan Club in the Hollywood area of Los Angeles.

"I remember the first time I ever played one of those back then," said Huckabee. "It was at G#sharp Music in Texarkana [Arkansas], and it was like butter to play! I knew it was one of those guitars that I wanted, but I couldn't afford it; they were priced out of my range."

However, the Ventures also played Fender instruments before and after their Mosrite affiliation, and founding guitarist Don Wilson (1933–2022) later teamed with his son Tim in a guitar business called Wilson Guitar Ventures, which marketed the Wilson Bros. brand.

To many observers, Wilson Bros. instruments did indeed draw a large portion of their design influences from Mosrite, right down to the angled neck/bass pickup and the German carve top on upgrade models. A VMB-75 bass was presented to Huckabee when the band played on his Fox News television show, abetted by the host on bass and members of the Little Rockers, the show's house band.

The instrument's signatures read—left to right—Nokie Edwards, Don Wilson, Leon Taylor, and Bob Spalding. Its sunburst finish was somewhat rare, as its profile on the Wilson Guitar Ventures website advertised the model in Candy Apple Red, Pearl White, and Metallic Blue. In a nod to the past, the pickguard has a barely perceptible mint green tint, as found on more than one brand of California-made guitars in the '60s.

The VMB-75 has an alder body and maple neck with 20 frets on a rosewood fingerboard, and the bass has a full 34-inch scale. Electronics include two FB-1 single-coil pickups, two volume controls, and a master tone knob.

It's very balanced and comfortable to play, and Mike was ebullient about not only his appearance with the band, but also his new bass as well.

"That one is a treasure," he enthused, "and it will always be a treasure. And there's no way that we can fully acknowledge the Ventures for their inspiration. If someone grew up in the '60s, they played a Ventures song if they were learning to play guitar—*every single one of us*. 'Walk, Don't Run,' 'Telstar,' others. That was the way you learned to play back then."

5. BEATLEMANIA FOREVER

As of this writing, Mike's Beatles fixation is still strong almost six decades after the band's appearance on *The Ed Sullivan Show*, so it's not a surprise that he has acquired numerous brands and models associated with that quartet.

Obviously, his 1964 Gretsch Tennessean would have an appropriate place in this lineup, but since that model was one of his personal guitars in the '70s, the replacement he acquired from Steve Evans in March 2003 is noted in the "Personal Time (Warp) Machines" chapter.

Huckabee has even zeroed in on an example of a pre-Beatles guitar associated with George Harrison.

EGMOND "BEGINNER'S GUITAR" MID-'50S

"A friend of mine who was a contractor knew I was a Beatles fanatic," Mike remembered, "and for some reason, he had bought that guitar years earlier. He was a Beatles fan, too, but not on the same level that I was. This one was very close to George's Egmond."

As a youngster, Harrison had reportedly attempted to build his own guitar around 1956, but if that primitive instrument still exists, its whereabouts are unknown. A Dutch-made Egmond "Beginner's Guitar"—its designation in an advertisement—was then purchased by Harrison.

The signed label inside of Mike's example reads, "The signature on this label guarantees that this instrument is a genuine Egmond guitar which passed minute final inspection for lasting satisfaction—Egmond Brothers Ltd, Holland—factory of musical instruments."

2011 RICKENBACKER 325C64

This brand and model is the most-cited Beatles instrument associated with John Lennon. Founded in the 1930s, the Rickenbacker company has been a family-owned business since the early '50s, building legendary instruments in Santa Ana, California, in a methodical, unhurried manner—no loud promotions or egregious hype.

The 325 has been made in several variations in its history, but the 325C64 is the enduring model, due to its Lennon connection (and those last two numbers in the model designation are a hint at the year the Beatles exploded on the international music scene). It's only available in a black finish called Jetglo.

The body is a semi-hollow style made of maple. The neck is also maple, and its rosewood fingerboard has 21 frets (all clear of the body) on a short-scale length of only 21 inches.

The three pickups are touted (and trademarked) as Vintage Single Coil Toaster Top units. The reference to the small kitchen appliance is a nod to the style of the chrome covers. The vibrato arm on this example has been removed.

2003 EPIPHONE CASINO

John Lennon played an Epiphone Casino model in the iconic rooftop concert that served as the finale of the 1970 Beatles documentary *Let It Be*. There's one major difference in that guitar and a similar-looking Casino owned by Huckabee—whereas Mike's guitar is a natural finished instrument that had been through a standard finishing process when it was built, Lennon had sanded the finish off his Casino, exposing the bare wood of the guitar body.

The Casino was the Epiphone equivalent of a Gibson ES-330, with a thinline maple body and two P-90 pickups. Other Gibson and Epiphone thinline models with similar silhouettes had a center block of wood inside, but the ES-330 and the Casino were hollow.

Paul McCartney and George Harrison also had Epiphone Casinos, and all three of those guitars figured into the recording of *Sgt. Pepper's Lonely Hearts Club Band* and other works.

The Beatles had been advised that a literally natural guitar body (sans paint, varnish, or lacquer) would sound better, and in mid-1968, while recording the two-disc "White Album" (the official title was simply *The Beatles*), Lennon and Harrison stripped the finishes off their respective Casinos.

In the ensuing decades, the Epiphone Casino has been popular in a natural-but-not-bare-wood finish due to the Beatles association. Huckabee is a stereotypical customer.

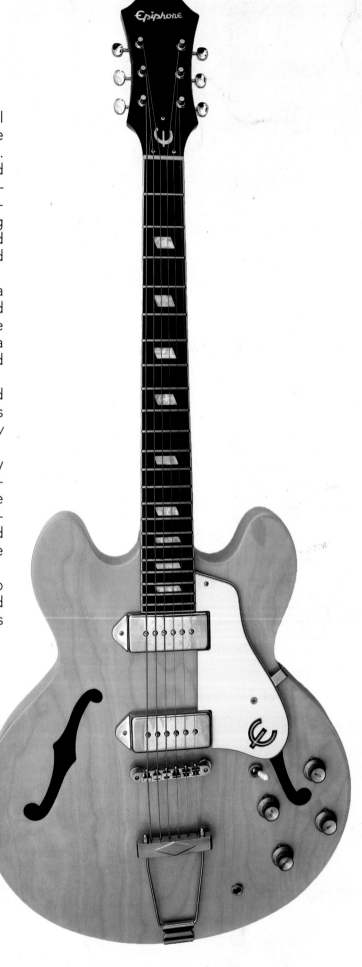

HOFNER HI SERIES B-BASS

No attempt to garner an assemblage of Beatles-related guitars, basses and memorabilia would be complete without a Hofner violin-shaped bass to reference Paul McCartney's legendary left-handed instrument (with a Beatles set list taped to its body), considered by some to be most valuable musical instrument in the world.

Over the decades, Hofner "Beatle basses" have been marketed in numerous configurations and at numerous price points.

Huckabee opted to buy a relatively inexpensive HI-Series B-Bass instrument that accomplishes the look and provides a decent sound.

The instrument is fully hollow and has a 30-inch scale. Obviously, it's very lightweight. A Hofner representative confirmed that the B-Bass is part of the company's "entry level" series. That said, it still has a spruce top, flame maple back and sides, and a maple neck and rosewood fingerboard. The Hofner rep stated that the HI B-Bass is capable of sounding like a double bass.

TANGENT: Huckabee's love of the Beatles has compelled him to make more than one pilgrimage to the band's hometown of Liverpool, England. In 2018, he and Janet met up in Liverpool with Debbie and Jeff Carlisi, who had flown to the UK for their daughter's wedding.

The Carlisis were fascinated by the legendary locations that had been referenced in Beatles songs, such as Penny Lane and Strawberry Fields. The Cavern Club is a surprisingly diminutive, cramped basement venue that is relatively unchanged since the days of Beatles performances there over 60 years ago.

The two couples also met two members of the Quarrymen, the skiffle group that John Lennon founded in 1956, which evolved into the Beatles.

"Colin Hanton was the Quarrymen's original drummer," Jeff detailed, "and Len Garry had joined in 1957, playing tea chest bass."

The Carlisis and the Huckabees also conversed with author Julia Baird, John Lennon's half-sister, whom Jeff described as "an excellent writer."

"We also had a lovely sit down with Freda Kelly, the Beatles' faithful and loyal secretary," Carlisi commented.

Left to right: Jeff Carlisi, Colin Hanton, Julia Baird, Mike, Len Garry—Courtesy of Jeff Carlisi.

6. ETC.

Not surprisingly, Huckabee has a separate music room at his home, where he and friends get together for occasional informal jam sessions. Most of his instruments are on display and interesting and/or improbable "schmooze" photos adorn the walls and bookshelves, showing Mike—and sometimes Janet as well—hanging out with unlikely acquaintances, such as Gene Simmons of Kiss.

In spite of being blessed with dozens of instruments that were given to him outright, Mike will still occasionally purchase instruments or gizmos that have tweaked his interest.

Huckabees with Gene Simmons—Courtesy of Mike Huckabee

2004 EPIPHONE MB-250 BANJO

"I bought that specifically to put in the music room," Huckabee said of the only banjo in his assemblage of instruments.

"I don't know how to play banjo. I bought it on an online auction site in the summer of 2021. When I found it online, I thought it would look really nice in the music room, but I *do* have some friends who will come over and want to try it out, so I'll be ready for them."

The Epiphone MB-250 was one of the better-grade banjos proffered in the company's Bluegrass collection. It has a maple rim and mahogany neck, and its extensive fretboard inlay and headstock decoration is eye-catching. Its scale is 26 1/4 inches.

EPIPHONE EL CAPITAN ACOUSTIC BASS

"I had just wanted an acoustic bass to play around with for my own enjoyment, if I felt like it," said Mike. "It was the first acoustic bass I ever had."

As noted earlier, the El Capitan acoustic bass is a step-up from the El Segundo bass. Mike had purchased this El Capitan prior to receiving an El Segundo model from Gibson.

The El Capitan sported an all-maple body that was akin to a Gibson J-200 acoustic guitar (and catalogs pointed out this distinction). It was originally available in a natural finish but later switched to a Vintage Sunburst finish. It started out with the same electronics as the El Segundo but ultimately switched to a fancier system known as the Shadow Classic P4 multi-band preamp.

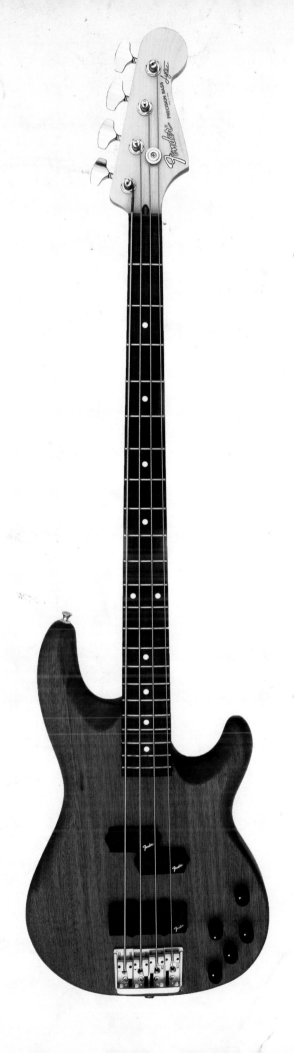

FENDER PRECISION BASS LYTE DELUXE, MID-'90S

Around the time he became governor, Huckabee noticed a new Fender bass model called the Precision Bass Lyte Deluxe in a Little Rock store called Boyd Music. He was attracted to the new bass, although he owned the white refinished Jazz Bass that Janet had recently found in a pawn shop.

"It had a mahogany, satin-finish body, so it was beautiful," he enthused. "It also played very nicely, it sounded wonderful, and it was lightweight. I was just getting back into guitars, just starting up with the church band. So, I bought it because it seemed to fit me so well. It was new, whereas the white Jazz Bass was used."

With its slightly downsized body, slim neck, Gotoh mini tuners, lighter weight, and easy playability, the standard Precision Bass Lyte lived up to its model name when it was introduced in 1992. The original P-Bass Lyte had gold-plated hardware, active circuitry, and a P/J pickup configuration. The four control knobs on a Precision Bass Lyte were not, as might have been expected, separate volume and tone for each pickup. Instead, there was a master volume knob, a pan knob, and separate bass and treble boost/cut controls.

The gold hardware moved over to the short-lived Precision Bass Lyte Deluxe model in 1995, and the standard model switched to chrome hardware. The Deluxe also featured a larger humbucking pickup in the bridge position and a fancier control system (an extra tone knob for midrange). The mahogany body was indeed offered in the 1995 catalog with a satin natural finish, and the specifications also cited a satin finish on the maple neck.

2012 FENDER-ROLAND G-5 VG STRATOCASTER

Advances in modeling technology have enabled certain guitars to sound like other musical instruments, and Fender teamed with the Roland company to develop and market a Stratocaster with high-end circuitry built into it. Mike's guitar, made in 2012, has a three-tone sunburst and rosewood fretboard, and those two small black knobs are capable of unleashing a myriad of tones and tunings.

The Tuning knob offers normal tuning, Drop D, Open G, D Modal, Baritone, and 12-string. The Mode knob is capable of cranking out the stereotypical sounds of a "normal" Stratocaster, modeled Stratocaster, modeled Telecaster, humbucking pickups, and acoustic.

The sonic possibilities seem to be almost endless. The hang-tag for the instrument's headstock touts "20 different instrument and pickup sounds." No special cable from guitar to amplifier is required.

"It has a multitude of variations," Huckabee enthused. "I saw one at the NAMM show, and thought it was really cool because it was one guitar that does it all. I met the CEO of Roland and bought one. The demo on it was amazing; someone had really worked it up great. You can make it sound like nylon strings on a classical (guitar).

"I don't play guitar all that much, but when I do, typically that's the one I pick up to fool around with because it's got a great feel, as well as so many different things to play with. If someone comes to my house and we're going to goof around in the music room, that guitar will usually get involved."

GLEN BURTON GE47

Talk about an attention-getting instrument—the Glen Burton GE47 was a replica of an AK-47 assault rifle, but it was also a complete and fully functional electric guitar.

It has a maple bolt-on neck, mahogany body, and rosewood fretboard. Electronics include two open-coil humbucking pickups, master volume and tone knobs, and a three-way pickup toggle switch. Black anodized hardware, including a vibrato, added to the military/stealth vibe. It was available in camouflage or black finishes. A competing brand offered a similar instrument in a desert sand color, referencing deployments by US forces in recent times.

"I found that over at Steve Evans's store over in Jacksonville," Mike said. "I just thought it was cool, and it was inexpensive. I showed it to Ted Nugent, and he approved."

Mike has relied on three primary basses to play on his television show, which is broadcast from what is now known as the Huckabee Theater on the grounds of the Trinity Music City complex in Hendersonville, Tennessee, a suburb of Nashville.

RICKENBACKER 4003

Almost every facet of this brand and model has a "classic" connotation. Fender basses were more popular than Rickenbackers, but the differences in the two brands were noticeable—visually, construction-wise, and sonically.

And Rickenbacker is also a California company, located not too far down the road from Fender's factory.

Whereas Fender basses had a bolt-on neck that was relatively easy to replace, Rickenbacker was the first solid-body electric bass manufacturer to successfully introduce neck-through bass construction with its 4000 series. After experimenting with walnut and mahogany in the first few years, the design evolved into almost-all-maple construction—the maple "wings" that were glued onto the center piece (also maple, with a thin walnut strip) formed a body with a memorable silhouette. The upper cutaway style has been called a "cresting wave," and its disproportionate size meant that the instrument is very comfortable and balanced.

The sound of a Rick bass is, to many players, one of a kind and unmistakable. Its resonance is almost piano-like, especially when the instrument is played with a pick. Famous bassists who have relied on Rickenbackers include Paul McCartney, Chris Squire of the Yes, Paul Goddard of the Atlanta Rhythm Section, and Ian "Lemmy" Kilmister of Motörhead.

Mike's Rickenbacker is a model 4003, made in 2008. It's a two-pickup model (the treble pickup is under the handrest). Its finish is a stan-

Onstage on the Huckabee Show—Courtesy TBN

dard (and classic) Rickenbacker color called Fireglo, a pink-to-crimson sunburst. Other standard finishes for the model over the decades have been Mapleglo (natural) and Jetglo (black). In more recent times, Midnight Blue has pretty much worked its way into standard status as well.

The governor opted for a Fireglo finish on his 4003 because it was close to what he termed a "Razorback Red" color. He admitted, however, that blue is his favorite finish.

Huckabee enjoys playing this bass on his show because its sound is unique and noticeable at almost any volume—it's equally at home for loud rockin' tunes or ballads.

"There's nothing else like them," he said.

TOBIAS FOUR-STRING

"When I was governor, my band was playing in Nashville," Huckabee recalled, "and we went to the Gibson factory. One of our guys was a stockbroker and was well off. He had bought several guitars that had been made at the Gibson Custom Shop, and he wanted to check on the status of one that he had ordered.

"I visited with [then-Gibson CEO] Henry Juszkiewicz. He knew that, at the time, I was playing that white Fender Jazz Bass that Janet had bought for me at a pawn shop.

"Henry said, 'You know, I think Gibson would like to see you playing a four-string Tobias,' and I still have it. It was out of the blue, totally unexpected. It's a wonderful instrument."

Gibson had bought the Baldwin Piano Company in 2001. The acquisition included a factory in Conway, Arkansas (in the greater Little Rock area) that measured 62,500 square feet. Baldwin pianos and Slingerland drums were still being built in the facility, but there was plenty of unused space. In addition to its Nashville factory, Gibson was building acoustic guitars in Memphis and Bozeman, Montana.

"A year or two after I got the Tobias bass, I was using it extensively when Henry told me that they were probably going to expand the Tobias line, and they'd probably do that in Memphis.

"I said, 'Henry, you're already building Baldwin pianos in Conway, Arkansas. There's no other governor in America playing a Tobias bass; why would you make them in Tennessee? My state can make you a nice incentive offer.'

"We got our industrial people together, and it happened. When that operation started up, Henry gave me the five-string Tobias bass."

Michael Tobias had founded his company in Orlando in 1977. His handcrafted basses were high-end instruments made from exotic tonewoods. Most of the instruments had natural, hand-rubbed finishes.

Gibson purchased Tobias in 1990, and the founder remained with the new owners until 1992, after which he founded the Michael Tobias Designs company.

Mike played his Tobias bass on the debut episode of his TBN show—Courtesy TBN

Huckabee's Tobias instruments are both "Classic" model basses, which had been in the Tobias lineup before the company's acquisition by Gibson. The style and sound of Tobias basses is oriented toward using multiple tonewoods that also look exquisite.

The five-piece multiple laminate neck-through design is asymmetrical and is "shaped to fit the contours of the human hand, which helps to eliminate muscle fatigue," according to a generic owner's manual for several Tobias models, including the Classic. On Mike's four-string, the primary neck-through wood is walnut, with contrasting purpleheart stringers/"stripes"; on the five-string, the neck-through portion is maple, also with purpleheart stringers.

The fingerboard has 24 frets and a 15-inch radius. The four-string has a quilted maple cap on the body, while the newer five-string has a flame maple cap.

The bridge and tuners were custom-made for Tobias.

Electronics consist of an active preamp for two humbucking Bartolini pickups. The upper two knobs control volume and pan, and the lower tone knobs are for treble, midrange, and bass. The mini-toggle switch is interesting—it's a tone bypass switch that does exactly that—the treble, midrange, and bass controls do not function, and the signal goes straight to the amplifier, allowing an alternate tone setting to be preset or controlled there.

Tobias basses were made in Conway for around ten years.

2012 WILKINS CLASSIC PERIOD CORRECT WRJT4

Peter Cetera, former bassist and vocalist for Chicago, forged a successful solo career after he departed from that band. He's responsible for gifting Huckabee with a Jazz Bass-style instrument crafted by a veteran luthier, and as of this writing, Cetera hasn't been on Mike's television show.

A longtime builder out of Van Nuys, California, Pat Wilkins recalled that he started building guitars in 1984, "but I didn't really get serious about it until 1990. At least 90 percent of my instrument builds are basses. I rarely build to stock because most players want to feel connected to my instruments through their designs. Even if it's a minor modification here or there, they're getting something specifically tailored for them."

Wilkins was playing in a band with Peter Cetera's brother, Kenny. The band's bass player, Joe Iaquinto, was playing a Wilkins bass, and an introduction to Peter resulted in Wilkins building a replica of a '60s Fender Precision Bass.

"Olympic White, maple and rosewood neck, and a tortoiseshell pickguard," Wilkins detailed. "I've been such a big fan of Peter that when the bass was done—and he was happy with it—I *gave* it to him, no charge. He was pretty surprised and gratefully accepted it. The next week he called me and asked me to build a bass for his friend Mike Huckabee. He insisted on paying for this one, and I took his money."

The build was coordinated by Cetera, and Pat crafted a model known as the Classic Period Correct WRTJ4.

"It's a completely standard model with no options," said Wilkins. "I was able to build this bass in about eight weeks."

Specifications on the instrument include an alder body, a two-piece maple neck, and vintage 6230 fretwire. The instrument is passive, and its pickups are Seymour Duncan SJB-1s.

Upon receiving the bass, Huckabee called the luthier to express his appreciation and sent Wilkins some political swag.

"I know he was happy with the bass," Wilkins summarized. "He uses it quite often. I'm incredibly proud to know that a man who twice made a bid to become our United States president thinks enough of it to keep it and use it."

Note: Mike is shown playing this WRJT4 Wilkins bass on the front cover

8. GUESTS AND THEIR GUITARS

The house band for the Huckabee show is Tré Corley and the Music City Connection. Each week, Corley and his musical associates work closely with guest artists during Friday afternoon rehearsals to craft viable musical arrangements for that evening's taping of the show. They're pros, and the results are always impressive.

It goes without saying that many of the musical guests on Huckabee's television show have also been guitar lovers and collectors, and they're always up for a conversation about classic guitar and bass models and classic sounds, including discussions about the music their own guitars and basses created.

Some of the instruments played on the broadcast have been with their owners for decades. Other guitars and basses may be newer, but those instruments offer exquisite tones and playability to enhance the present-day presentation. Either way, their owners are usually proud to show them off and detail their use.

Accordingly, several musicians enthusiastically agreed to profile the guitars and basses they've used in Hendersonville, on performances that were seen and heard around the world.

Bandleader Tré Corley with a formidable musical guest, legendary bassist Victor Wooten—Courtesy TBN

DOYLE DYKES

Having first come to notice in the gospel music field with the Stamps Quartet, Doyle Dykes's powerful, melodic guitar work has made him a respected "player's player" for decades. Other famous musicians are often stunned by Dykes's prowess—a definitive example of his jaw-dropping talent is his Warp Ten rendition of "Wabash Cannonball."

James Burton is so much of a Dykes fan that Doyle is the only guitarist who was invited to play at every James Burton International Guitar Festival in Shreveport, Louisiana, starting in 2005.

For his appearance on the Huckabee show, Doyle relied on his signature Guild guitar, a flat-top acoustic with a pointed Florentine cutaway. Dykes imparted the details:

"The Guild is a spectacular instrument, with an Adirondack (spruce) top and bracing, and a reinforced multi-ply neck. it is slightly thinner than the other Guild guitars in its shape, which causes it to be quick and very responsive. The amazing maple body also allows it to cut through like a solo singer. It really stands out and carries the orchestral dynamics well without distorting.

"The LR Baggs LB-6 pickup allows it to sound louder and more full, acoustically. I also love the 25 1/4-inch scale; it's perfect!"

Perhaps not surprisingly, Doyle performed a tune that's a favorite of his as well as his fans, "Guitar Poor," with Mike and the house band. It's a fun song with which almost any guitar collector can relate.

"'Guitar Poor' was definitely a band tune," the guitarist said, "and I looked forward to playing with Tré and his great band, and I especially wanted to pick alongside the governor!"

The deeply spiritual guitarist described his appearance on the Huckabee show as "an answer to prayer.... It was a great experience from the time I pulled into the parking to the time I left. It was a 'God thing.'"

Dykes was asked if stereotypical Huckabee audiences would continue to appreciate his music if he made a return appearance on the show.

"I would hope so," he replied. "I would love to do 'Wabash Cannonball' although I typically play it solo.

"I was so glad I got to be on the governor's show because I think his show has opened up a whole new audience. I'm thankful to TBN and have been a fan for years. Bringing the Huckabee show onboard was a brilliant idea that definitely reaches a wider audience."

Doyle on the set of the Huckabee show with his Guild signature guitar.—Courtesy TBN

MARK FARNER

Founding guitarist for Grand Funk Railroad, Michigan native Mark Farner has garnered worldwide acclaim. Earlier in his career, he participated in the stereotypical wild rock-and-roll lifestyle that accompanied such fame. He had a "born again" experience in the mid-'80s and set out in a different musical direction, purveying rock music with a Christian vibe, as well as selected Grand Funk songs that were appropriate for traditional-values listeners.

A relatively brief reunion for the original members of Grand Funk Railroad transpired in the mid-'90s, and Farner also played with ad hoc nostalgia aggregations like Ringo's All-Starr Band and the 2002 edition of the "A Walk Down Abbey Road" tour. As of this writing, he's still got an active solo career and maintains a faith-based musical approach, although his shows still include plenty of Grand Funk hits.

After having been a Peavey endorser for a number of years, Farner

Mark's hardtail Parker Fly guitar has been his primary performance guitar since the mid-90s.—Courtesy TBN

was compelled to find a lightweight guitar in the mid-'90s, following serious surgery on his spine. He recounted that a piece of bone from a cadaver was implanted in his neck.

A then-new guitar line, Parker, featured lightweight instruments made from modern composite materials, and their Fly model only weighed about 4 1/2 pounds. Mark has counted on a red Parker Fly, which he nicknamed "Baby," as his go-to instrument ever since he acquired it. Baby also has a sister guitar named Ruby, and both instruments are hardtails (no vibrato system).

Like a lot of utility instruments, Mark's guitar has been decorated with stickers. A closer look at the body reveals that the brighter red images are silhouettes of the Great Lakes.

"Baby is showing off her devotion to my home state," Farner detailed. "The red-and-white round sticker was given to me by an artist I met on the road. . . . The stickers on the lower horn above each end of her name are American flags—one says, 'Thank you for my freedom,' and the other says, 'Honor our heroes.'"

A small cross has been attached to the upper cutaway horn, as seen previously on two of Mark's Peavey guitars that he had been using prior to his surgery. The cross was the first item Farner placed on the Parker guitar; the stickers came later.

"It is not the same cross from one of my Peavey Impacts," said the veteran guitarist, "but it represents my same Savior."

THE KENTUCKY HEADHUNTERS

Formerly known as Itchy Brother, a longhaired blues/rock aggregation called the Kentucky Headhunters stormed out of Glasgow in the south central part of that state into the already evolving country music scene in 1989. Their appropriately titled *Pickin' On Nashville* album included rollicking cover versions of songs like Bill Monroe's "Walk Softly On This Heart Of Mine" and Henson Cargill's "Skip A Rope," among others.

"Steve Earle, Dwight Yoakam, the Georgia Satellites, and Foster & Lloyd had opened the doors for us," said lead guitarist Greg Martin. "While there were still elements of the old country music guard in place at that time, it was a very exciting time, musically. The album brought a wide group of folks together in 1989. We've been blessed."

Pickin' On Nashville turned out to be a Grammy-winning effort. The 'Heads realized that by straddling musical genres, they were onto something, and their style was still serving them well nearly a third of a century later, when they appeared on the Huckabee show in late 2021.

It wasn't surprising that the band brought along some cool instruments. Greg is a consummate tone hound, and he relies on classic guitars, such as his 1958 Gibson Les Paul Standard and 1957 Fender Stratocaster, in the studio. He used a viable retro-style guitar for the TBN appearance.

"I played my 2014 Gibson Custom Shop Ronnie Montrose CC #28 Les Paul reissue," he said. "It feels very similar to my '58 Les Paul."

Bassist/vocalist Doug Phelps has relied on a 1958 Fender Precision Bass as his primary instrument for decades.

"I bought it in 1987 from Sumner County Music in Gallatin, Tennessee," said Phelps. "I recorded with that one on every Headhunters record, and I still play it at all of our live shows. It's my go-to bass in the studio, on the road, and on any radio or TV broadcast."

The vintage P-Bass also had other fans backstage.

"Both Mike Huckabee and [house band bassist] Lorie Sikes were interested in my old '58!" Phelps recalled with a chuckle. "Right before we went on stage to perform, Mike was backstage with us, and the first thing he asked about was my old 1958 P-Bass!"

Richard Young usually relies on a 1952 Fender Telecaster he's nicknamed "Danny" (after late guitarist Danny Gatton) in the studio. For the TBN

Stringed instrument members of the band are—left to right—Greg Martin, Doug Phelps, and Richard Young. Drummer Fred Young can be seen in the rear, between Martin and Phelps.—Courtesy TBN

broadcast, he brought a custom-made Tele-style guitar made by luthier Charles Whitfill of Lebanon, Kentucky, and a vintage Gibson ES-335TDC. He's lusted after 335s for decades.

"I got my first 335 in 1968," said Young. "I've always gravitated to them when the 'Heads go into a total blues mode or Chuck Berry vibe.

"There is something about the hollow, woody sound and the bounce-back response you get when playing a good one. It's like they speak a foreign language that no one can understand but the player. I'm quite sure the guys that played them constantly—like B. B. King, Freddie King, Alvin Lee, Chuck, and all the folks who played similar hollow bodies through the years—could attest to that vibe. It's like you and the guitar meld into one. As the rhythm guitar for the 'Heads, I rarely take a lead solo; I leave that to Greg, but when I strap on the 335, I become a different animal, and I step up to the plate to play double solos with him, and I create my own solos onstage. That's something I don't do much with a solid-body electric.

"The red 335 I'm now playing is a 1970, which belonged to a fellow in Louisville, Kentucky, who played it in a church."

The Kentucky Headhunters' stage setup also features Fred Young's unique percussion ensemble, which interpolates vintage marching band drums. The array always gets attention from fans and other musicians (as do Fred's sideburns), and the Huckabee show gig was no exception. Richard pronounced the drum kit "the centerpiece of our stage show. It fits the 'Heads sound and image."

The interaction between the Headhunters, Huckabee, and the Music City Connection was a positive experience all the way around.

"Huckabee was great," said Greg. "He's a wonderful host, and his ability to transcend politics and talk music was appreciated. He's also a fan of vintage instruments. We were talking about that even off-camera. I have nothing but praise for the governor, his staff, and his house band. Even the snacks in the dressing room were superb!"

Doug was appreciative of the audience's reactions to the songs they performed.

"We received a great response," the bassist said. "'Dumas Walker' still gets the crowd going to this day, and it's certainly one of our staple songs. We're glad we wrote that one!

"Mike has a great rapport with his audience and is very personable with his guests. He has a very talented house band, and they can cover any genre."

"We played our first and only Christmas song, 'Let's All Get Together And Fight,'" Young remembered, "and when we went off the air, Mike leaned over and asked me, 'Did you write that song about my family?'

"Being on his show was the real deal. His being a musician and his knowledge of music made it very special for us. He and I are the same age, so it was like talking with someone I had grown up with."

Summing up, Martin waxed philosophical about the band's ongoing efforts, even as members reach retirement age (and it helps to know that Richard's son is playing drums for a successful band called Black Stone Cherry).

"When we hit it back in 1989, I had already been on the road ten years," he said. "I figured by the time I hit 60, if I was lucky, I'd be done. I'm now 69 and still at it, which amazes me! I never pondered the future as a teenager or young adult; I just took it one day at a time and hoped for the best. The Lord sure has taken good care of His four little ragamuffins.

"I believe the audiences, including the Huckabee audience, get a bigger kick seeing we're still at it after all these years. Bring on the Geritol!"

VINCE MARTELL

Vince Martell, lead guitarist for the Vanilla Fudge, has been through numerous brands and models of guitars since that band exploded on the music scene in 1967 with a formidable "artsy"/almost avant-garde reworking of the Supremes' "You Keep Me Hanging On." Many students of popular music history have pronounced the innovative band from Long Island, New York the founders of what came to be known as progressive rock. That category ultimately included bands like Yes, Kansas, and Emerson, Lake & Palmer. Even Deep Purple acknowledged being influenced by the Fudge.

The Vanilla Fudge still gigs on occasion (bassist Tim Bogert died in early 2021), and Martell also has a solo career. He uses his present-day frontline instrument with all his musical projects.

"The guitar is part of my endorsement," he said. "It is a Dean Deceiver, but I don't like that name, so I call it the Defender, as in US Navy veteran."

(NOTE: Martell is a US Navy veteran.)

Modifications to the guitar include a conversion from active circuitry to passive, replacement pickups, and a coil splitter switch.

The instrument's body and neck are mahogany, and the binding on the top of the body includes abalone pearl. The ebony fretboard has 24 frets with seagull inlays and is slightly scalloped.

"I did it," Martell said of the scalloping, "because I prefer digging into the fretboard when I bend, sustain, and shake the strings."

Like Farner's Parker Fly, Martell's Dean Deceiver/Defender has been custom decorated.

"The '427' number is a reference to the engine in my '68 'Vette I had during the Fudge's biggest days. Five hundred horsepower, and it *moved* . . . and by the way, I never lost a race."

Stick-on letters spell out "Save the animals," "Save the treez" (*sic*), and "Jesus Loves Uz" (*sic*)—Martell recalled with a laugh that he ran out of 'S' stickers.

Courtesy TBN

There's also a patriotic U.S.A. sticker and a small white image that is "a fleur-de-lis reminiscent of royalty and Christian hierarchy," according to Vince.

Martell praised the look of the Huckabee Theater's stage and the efforts of the show's house band in backing him on his original composition, "Life Runneth Free."

"The set is beautiful," he said "It has a reverent vibe. Almost church-like, with the stained glass.

"Tré Corley and his band were great, and Gov. Mike did a masterful job on his Rickenbacker. All of the people behind the scenes also treated me like royalty, and the audience was warm and receptive. God bless them all."

STEVE WARINER

Winner of four Grammy awards, Indiana native Steve Wariner also has the distinction of having been awarded a rare and coveted Certified Guitar Player (CGP) citation from the legendary Chet Atkins.

And he's also developed a strong friendship with Mike Huckabee.

"The first time I met the governor was in Indianapolis—my backyard—at a governor's conference where I played," Wariner remembered. "He was the first person to introduce himself to me. He let me know he was a bass player, which was what I had started on with Dottie West and Bob Luman and Chet."

Wariner has been on Huckabee's show more than once and has performed with the governor on other occasions. Two TV appearances happened in 2020, during the COVID-19 quarantine. The first was on June 6, and it was a given that he would sing his hit "Holes in the Floor of Heaven" on the show.

"That was right in the middle of the 'hard lockdown,'" said Steve. "Off-camera, the governor, me, and everybody else were wearing masks and giving each other space, but we all got through it."

In November of the same annum, he returned to the show to perform a song with the legendary Jeannie Seely called "If You Could Call It That." The composition of that song had been started by Dottie West decades earlier, and it was completed in recent times by Wariner and Bobby Tomberlin. Seely had included the song on her new album. The Huckabee episode on which it was performed included an appearance by Bill Anderson.

Wariner's guitar of choice for his appearances on the Huckabee show was a unique Gibson Hummingbird acoustic.

"It's part of Gibson's antiquity series," he explained. "It looks and feels like an old vintage Hummingbird. The guys at Gibson's factory out in Montana make those guitars the old-style way, to old specs. It's incredible; I've had it for many years now and it's one of my favorites."

Wariner has his own record label (SelecTone) and also has a signature model Gretsch electric guitar. One of Chet Atkins's signature Gretsch models had been called the Country Gentleman, and Wariner's model is known as the Nashville Gentleman.

"I thought it was a cool name because Chet was my mentor and hero," he said. "It was designed by my son Ryan and myself and a great

Courtesy TBN

guitar maker named Jeff Senn. It took us almost two years to complete, including going through the prototypes. Gretsch was wonderful; they gave me carte blanche, and I'll be forever grateful for that because it's exactly the guitar that I wanted.

"If I ever played it on the Huckabee show, I would probably play something like 'Four Bus Breakdown,' one of the instrumental guitar pieces that I wrote; we actually had four buses break down on tour one time.

"Or maybe a song I wrote called 'The Nashville Gentleman,' named after the guitar.

"Or maybe a Chet song."

Wariner appreciates the opportunities he has had on the Huckabee show.

"They treat you right," he said. "I love the fact that he's a real player. I also like the fact that he's open about his faith and doesn't back down."

These days, Mike Huckabee stays active with his television program and other appearances in media. He's tapered back a bit from regularly attending NAMM shows but has always enjoyed examining and playing new instruments (particularly basses).

"I was on the NAMM Foundation's board for several years," he said, "which endeavors to get musical instruments to kids; I had been doing that in Arkansas, and I partnered with NAMM for a while to do it nationally."

There are only three instruments in Mike's collection that were custom ordered with his input. There's the reissue of the '70s Fender Jazz Bass that Steve Evans modded slightly to resemble Mike's original late '60s/early '70s Jazz Bass, the Overture bass, and the Wilkins bass. The other custom-made instruments were surprise gifts.

Asked about instrument specifications if he was to order another custom-built bass for himself, Huckabee paused, then said, "I'd certainly want a fast, slim neck. I'd probably want the tuners all on one side; I like the Fender style. Part of the reason is because when I clip a tuner onto the headstock, I like it on the bottom because it's easier to read and it doesn't compete with the keys on the top side. Having the keys on the top also means there's no doubt about which string you're turning. I'd also want two pickups—bass and treble—with easy switching capability. I like electronics on instruments to be simple; I don't need a lot of fancy stuff."

Huckabee was asked about a fantasy scenario in which he had to choose one of two basses, either his vintage 1962 Jazz Bass (which has some noticeable wear) or the specially ordered pristine recreation of his late '60s/early '70s Jazz Bass, which is much less expensive than its forebear from the early '60s.

"The '62," he replied immediately, "because it has history, it has character, and it has a rich tone. I just think an old guitar that's seasoned out—where the wood has totally reached its maturity—is going to have a magic sound and feel. If it's got nicks and road rash, that's part of the character. There's a story there. When I play my '62, I'm not just playing an instrument, I'm presenting its history as well. I think the stories behind a lot of these instruments are as valuable as the instruments themselves."

In the mid-1990s, one rock star who has a notable assemblage of instruments told *Vintage Guitar Magazine*, "My collection is like an amoeba, it's constantly changing shape." While Huckabee has acquired and turned instruments like any stereotypical collector, these days he considers himself to be "very much" saturated and satiated with his collection, so the transitory "shape" of his collection will most likely change less often . . . but it *will* change (and that "can't completely let go" attitude is probably true for any veteran collector). One wonders how many other Baby Boomer guitar collectors have been in the same frame of mind as they have entered retirement age.

That said, one of the more recent items he acquired was a vintage Sears Silvertone 1466 amplifier from the eBay auction site. It's the model that he first got when he switched to playing a Vox Clubman Bass.

And while recalling his decades of pawn-shopping for basses and guitars brings a bemused and/or nostalgic smile to Mike's face, nowadays he doesn't feel compelled to frequent such establishments as often. But he has enjoyed the ride for decades.

"I'm not really in an aggressive acquisition mode," he chuckled. "The only thing I'm trying to acquire at this point is a Clubman [bass]. I might *want* it, but I don't *need* it, obviously. If I ever came across an old Vox Strat-like guitar, I might pick it up, but it's not as important to me as the Clubman. Nothing else is out there that makes me say, 'Man, I really want that guitar.' There's no lust for them now.

"Maybe that '62 Jazz Bass is like Rosebud, the sled in [Orson Welles' 1941 movie] *Citizen Kane*. The Jazz Bass and the Gretsch Tennessean that I had to sell represented a sacrifice on my part in a time of my life when I didn't have a choice; I had to give them up.

"And did I need that Silvertone bass amp I got off of eBay? Heck, no. I've turned it on twice. I got it so it would remind me of when I was 12 or 13 years old.

"Anything else is gravy these days."

Billy has four guitars.
Suzy has one bass.
What does Suzy have that Billy doesnt?

A gig.
Suzy has a gig.

AFTERWORD AND ACKNOWLEDGMENTS

Yep, this one was definitely different, considering the type of collection that Gov. Huckabee has opted to assemble over the years.

The initial ideas regarding how to profile and display his assortment of basses and guitars (which included a number of "Everyman" instruments) produced a bit of head scratching, but Mike's egalitarian approach proved to be refreshing and workable…at least, for him and me.

The instruments the governor has opted to accumulate are indeed relatable for average folks, and perhaps the autographed instruments are definitive examples of such egalitarianism—he's a fan of certain bands and guitarists, just like umpteen other music buffs. Moreover, a lot of the general population may not know about the unheralded yet extremely talented builders who are meticulously designing and crafting exquisite guitars and basses in small shops full of sawdust all across America. Maybe this book will help give them some well-deserved attention.

I'm grateful that numerous luthiers, musicians, company representatives, and instrument enthusiasts agreed to work with me on this project.

But once again, the first person to acknowledge is my life partner, Gail, for her ongoing support. Our daughter Elizabeth gets a nod this time around, as well. I love both of you very much, and always will.

The folks at TBN—Tim Hart, Kris Rae, Pamela Case and maybe some folks behind the scenes with whom I didn't directly communicate—need to be cited for their courtesy and professionalism regarding archival photographs. Their images made a big difference in this book.

Other individuals who need to be noted for their assistance, research, image contributions and input include (in alphabetical order): Hogan Barker, James Burton, Jeff Carlisi, Brendan Duff, Karl Dustman, Doyle Dykes, Steve Evans, Mark Farner, Robert Floyd, Rudy Gatlin, Dan Hagar, John Harjo, Justin Hoffman, David Huckabee, Janet Huckabee, Wayne Jarrett, Kevin Johnson, Gwenn Levine, Brad Mader, Vince Martell, Greg Martin, Brady Muckelroy, Doug Phelps, Ash Reyes Picache, Steve Ridinger, Jim "My Favorite Mellotron Player" Shaw, Fiona Taylor, Chris Truong, Steve Wariner, Pat Wilkins, Vincent Wynne, Richard Young.

Thanks to Alan Greenwood at *Vintage Guitar Magazine* for the ongoing writing opportunity, now in its thirty-fourth year as of this writing.

And here's the interminable "read-between-the-lines" salute to the Messrs. Spilman for encouraging me to become a full-time writer. That 150-mile dogleg off of I-81 in early 2019 was worth it.

Obviously, the primary acknowledgement goes to Gov. Mike Huckabee for this opportunity. His focus, professionalism and eloquence were very much appreciated, and I did my best to reciprocate in a similar manner in our collaboration. We're both traditional regarding our faith, and our adherence to such principles underlined our commitment to collaborate on this presentation in an efficient manner. And that's exactly what we did.

What's more, the research for information regarding some of the instruments averred that the spirit of innovation is still viable when it comes to stringed musical instruments—the Cupit travel guitar and the U-Bass-FS are exemplary.

The governor is spot-on with his rumination about how a lot of guitars—new, autographed, used, vintage—have a lot of intriguing stories behind them. Some of those chronicles can be told, but others will remain untold forever. That's part of the mystique.

And maybe that's the way it ought to be.

—W.G.M.

BIBLIOGRAPHY AND REFERENCES

BOOKS

Evans, Steve and Ron Middlebrook. *Cowboy Guitars*. Anaheim Hills, CA: Centerstream Publishing, 2002.

Greenwood, Alan and Gil Hembree. *The Official Vintage Guitar Price Guide2021*. Bismarck, ND, Vintage Guitar Books, 2021.

Gruhn, George and Walter Carter. *Gruhn's Guide to Vintage Guitars: An Identification Guide For American Fretted Instruments* (Third Edition), Milwaukee: Backbeat Books, 2010.

Lamb, W. Scott. *Huckabee: The Authorized Biography*. Nashville, TN. W Publishing, 2015.

Moseley, Willie G. *Bakersfield Guitars: The Illustrated History*. Lanham, MD: Backbeat Books, 2021.

Petersen, David and Dick Denney. *The Vox Story: A Complete History of the Legend*. Westport, CT. The Bold Strummer, Ltd., 1993.

Scott, Jay. *The Guitars Of The Fred Gretsch Company*. Fullerton, CA: Centerstream Publishing, 1992.

PERIODICAL AND ONLINE ARTICLES

Babiuk, Andy. "The Beatles' Casinos." *Vintage Guitar Magazine*, May 2010.

Moseley, Willie G. "Jon Butcher: Land of the Midnight Sun, California Sun." *Vintage Guitar Magazine*, October, 1995.

Moseley, Willie G. "Phil Volk: Forever Fang." *Vintage Guitar Magazine*, June, 2004.

WEBSITES

baldwinpiano.com
bouldercreekguitars.com
guitarinsite.nl
kalabrand.com
musetechnical.com
notreble.com
rickenbacker.com
silvertoneworld.net
strictly-country.com
www.strumstick.com
www.vintageguitarandbass.com
vintaxe.com

ABOUT THE AUTHOR

A stereotypical Baby Boomer who loves guitars, Willie G. Moseley is the Senior Writer for *Vintage Guitar* magazine and news editor emeritus for *The Tallassee Tribune*. He resides with his family in rural Alabama ("Hank Williams Territory," he says). This is his fifteenth book.

Founded in 1986 by Alan Greenwood, Vintage Guitar is the world's longest continuously-owned guitar magazine.

SMOKE JUMPER, MOON PILOT
THE REMARKABLE LIFE OF APOLLO 14 ASTRONAUT STUART ROOSA
By Willie G. Moseley

Al Shepard was returning to the cosmos, and this time, he was going to walk on the Moon.

Grounded for most of the Sixties due to an inner ear problem, America's first man in space had been serving as NASA's Chief of the Astronaut Office, and had figured into the selection of crews for American manned space flights. Now healthy and cleared for flight himself, Shepard knew who he wanted on his own Apollo crew.

For Lunar Module Pilot, he selected a brilliant Navy aviator, Edgar Mitchell, a.k.a. "The Brain," who already had a doctorate of science in Aeronautics and Astronautics from M.I.T., and had been highly involved in the design of the Lunar Module.

The Command Module Pilot, who would be responsible for guiding the Apollo spacecraft to the Moon, placing it in a safe orbit, and returning it safely to Earth, was to be Air Force pilot Stuart Roosa.

And Roosa didn't even have a college degree when he had won his Air Force wings, and hadn't been on a backup crew for an Apollo flight.

But when it came to piloting skills, he was that good.

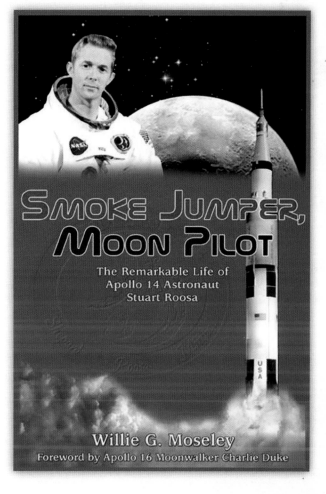

Stu Roosa's life was incredibly diverse—the second son of a government surveyor, he had spent his early childhood in a migratory lifestyle with his family before the Roosas settled in Claremore, Oklahoma, where Stu proved to be an excellent student and developed a lifelong love of hunting.

He became a smoke jumper for the Forest Service before enlisting in the Air Force's aviation cadet program. Excelling in piloting skills, Roosa had graduated from test pilot school at the legendary Edwards Air Force Base before being chosen as an astronaut.

Roosa loved his family and his country, and he loved to fly. Recollections in this detailed biography include memories from family members, schoolmates, and veteran smoke jumpers, pilots, and astronauts.

Smoke Jumper, Moon Pilot tells the story of a focused, determined, and patriotic youngster who believed in the American dream, and grew up to live it. At the age of 19, Stu Roosa was parachuting into the woods of the Pacific Northwest to fight forest fires.

— He joined the Air Force.
— He became a test pilot at Edwards Air Force Base.
— He was selected to be an astronaut by NASA.
— He went to the Moon.
— He became a successful businessman and big game hunter.

This is the family-authorized biography of Apollo 14 Command Module Pilot Stuart A. Roosa (1933-1994). It's the quintessential, All-American chronicle of the life of an Oklahoma farm boy whose initiative, drive and personal integrity earned him a place among the 24 individuals who made the most dramatic voyage in human history, and it's a story that needs to be told, now more than ever.

6x9, 256 pages, softbound, $24.95
ISBN: 978-1-956027-07-5

50 YEARS OF EXILE
THE STORY OF A BAND IN TRANSITION
By Randy Westbrook

Exile is a band with a diverse history. The group formed in 1963 looking to play small clubs in Richmond, Kentucky, but managed to top both the pop and the country charts during a ten-year span in the late 1970s and 1980s. "Kiss You All Over" was a major hit in 1978, spending four weeks at the top of Billboard's pop chart. After several less successful follow-up singles, the band decided to make a move to country music. This resulted in 10 number one country hits. All of this success led to an induction into the Kentucky Music Hall of Fame in 2013.

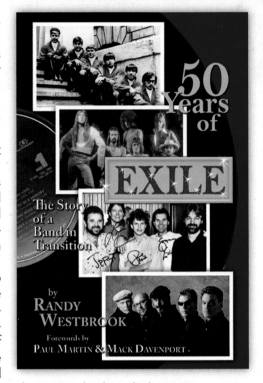

The years leading up to the release of "Kiss You All Over" represent an important and often misunderstood period in the band's history. During this time they played on three of Dick Clark's Caravan of Stars tours, released a series of singles and two full-length albums, worked with Tommy James, and played all over the Central Kentucky area and beyond. This book pays close attention to that era. In addition, a talented group of Kentucky musicians helped to rejuvenate the band in the 1990s, and this book tells their stories as well.

This is a "must read" for aspiring young musicians and anyone who has been touched by the music of Exile. It shows how talent must be combined with patience, bull-dogish-stick-to-it-tive-ness, a willingness to put in the hard work that is needed to work in the music industry, and, in many cases, luck. Several people have been a part of Exile, and each member contributed in different ways. They each have a separate story, but this is the story of a band. Exile is an entity held together. This book gives a thorough history, but it is an unfinished story because the band plays on.

6x9-inch, 272 pages, hardbound, $24.95
ISBN: 978-1-938905-22-3

ACTION UNLIMITED: THE BAND OF GOLD
A KENTUCKY BAND'S MUSICAL JOURNEY TO THE EDGE OF STARDOM
By Dewey Pope

In the Sixties, when Rock 'n' Roll exploded, there were thousands of bands. They dreamed of making it big, but most never got past playing in their garage. Some were good enough to play an occasional gig for pay at a wedding, a VFW hall or even a small local club. Even fewer played for pay regularly, with the prospect that music might become a career rather than a hobby. And then, there were those who were talented enough—and fortunate enough to be heard by the right people—who got the opportunity to take their shot at the big time.

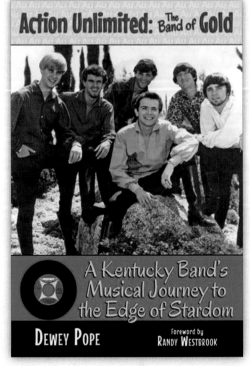

One of those talented and fortunate bands called themselves Action Unlimited. Having made a name for themselves in Richmond, Kentucky, the sextet caught the eyes and ears of associates of Dick Clark's organization, got a spot on the bill of one of Clark's Caravan of Stars shows, and linked up with a manager who had the connections to book them into the best nightclubs on the West Coast and Las Vegas.

The drummer of Action Unlimited, Dewey Pope, tells the story of the band's ascent to the upper echelon of rock bands in *Action Unlimited: The Band of Gold*. Pope shares with readers the band's evolution, their adventures (and misadventures) on the road, their coming-of-age experiences, their brushes with celebrities, and stories about sharing the stage and meeting some of the biggest names in music in the Sixties. Ride along with Action Unlimited in their tour vehicle—a gold-painted funeral hearse—and wax nostalgic as you share in their musical journey that took them to the threshold of stardom—so close that they could taste it—only to be denied entry. Join Dewey and bandmates Jon, Kent, Dave, Chuk and Sam and enjoy the story of a Kentucky band that almost made it big.

6x9-inch, 176 pages, hardbound, $24.95
ISBN: 978-1-942613-73-2

INDEX